GRAB THE KIDS & GO

A Practical Guide to your Family's Gap Year

TARYN ASH

WHAT YOU'LL FIND INSIDE!

Taryn Ash and her husband, Sam, pulled their 7th and 8th grade children out of school to explore 12 countries on four continents over several glorious months. They feasted on sweet mangos in Thailand, local grasses and barks in Laos, rubbery cobra in Vietnam and roasted warthog in Zimbabwe. As volunteers in South Africa, they worked hands-on to rehabilitate orphaned monkeys, collected wildlife data for academic research and tended to a wounded wild black rhino. In Zimbabwe, they taught English to youngsters, assisted residents in an elderly persons' home and worked in a garden benefiting victims of HIV/AIDs. They were taught how to make fire and catch guinea fowl by San Bush people of the Kalahari Desert, sat breathlessly under the stars as wild elephants greeted each other by a watering-hole, frolicked with playful children of the Himba tribe and attended a Herero tribal wedding in Nambia. They studied Buddhist meditation with a monk in rural Laos, struggled to kiteboard in the Philippines, explored the Vietnamese Mekong Delta by bicycle and boat, splashed their way through underground caves speckled with florescent worms in New Zealand and worked on restoring an ancient house in France. And that's not all.

This is book one of a two-book series written specially for parents who dream of discovering the world with their kids, but are overwhelmed by seemingly insurmountable obstacles. This practical guide tackles fears that stop families from fulfilling their travel dreams. It offers recommendations, logistical advice and answers to questions from: How to design the ideal itinerary, to how to have your home and pets cared for in your absence. Peppered throughout are words of wisdom from other well-travelled parents who have made exploring the world an integral feature of their families' lives.

Table of Contents

Chapter 1
The Big Leap

TEACHING AT CHINO TIMBA PRE-SCHOOL WITH MRS NYATHI WAS ONE OF THE TRUE HIGHLIGHTS OF OUR FAMILY'S GAP YEAR.
ZIMBABWE

Just a few short months before starting work on this book, my husband, Sam, and I began a life-changing conversation in which we questioned how our lives were meeting our expectations. By all traditional middle-class standards, we were doing just fine, with our comfortable house in a lovely Houston neighborhood, a good school for our kids, cars, cable TV and credit cards. But it was not us, and we knew it. We were hungry for adventure. The days seemed to be speeding past as we were crushed under the mundane sameness of shopping, homework and local restaurants.

We also recognized that the years would soon begin taking their toll on our bodies, our physical stamina, our enthusiasm for risk-taking, and our dreams of trekking the Himalayas and kite boarding in the Philippines might be left unrealized.

Perhaps our most profound realization was that the relationships we were having with our kids were not as we imagined they should be at this point. Our son, Declan, age 13 at the time and Scout, our daughter, just 12, were attending a well-regarded school that, like many American schools, was putting a worrying level of pressure on the kids to *perform*. This meant that there was virtually no time for a relaxing family life as homework deadlines ate into our evenings and weekends. Soon the kids would be moving on and we would look back on those years as a blur of tension and stress. It had become clear that it was time to *grab the kids and go!*

Adventure was what we were after, conversations with people from diverse worlds, exposure to new and different environments. Even a bit less comfort occasionally would make things more interesting. We were concerned by how much our kids were being shaped as consumers, defining themselves by what they owned rather than what they knew or had done for themselves or for other people, and that their day-to-day world was making them less physical and more risk-averse than Sam and I had been raised to be. We had learnt long ago that finding ourselves in new situations in unfamiliar places helps to build confidence and resourcefulness, and fills a life with precious memories. And that's what we wanted for our kids.

So, we decided to take the leap, pull the kids out of school, put work on hold, and set off to see the world for a few months, quietly hoping that the experience would bring us closer as a family, and nearer to the people Sam and I knew our true selves to be.

WHY THIS BOOK?

This book was an unexpected outcome of my family's around-the-world tour. Sam is actually the former journalist in the family, and I had quietly expected that his interest in writing would be rekindled while we travelled. It turned out that the interest was ignited in me.

While sitting on the porch of our bamboo hut overlooking the Mekong Delta, I began responding to messages from family and friends who had been following our journey through Facebook. Questions kept coming in about how we made this happen, and if I was writing a blog to teach other families how to do it. It was only then that I began to recognize the tremendous amount of knowledge I had acquired to make this ambitious tour happen. The planning process for this trip had taught me a lot, but the learning started over thirty years earlier when my journey as a global traveller began. Without that considerable know-how, I am not sure that we would have pulled this family world tour off as well as we did in such a short period. Or at all.

The truth was that I had the confidence to move full steam ahead with organising almost every detail of our rather complex world tour in just four short months. As soon as Sam was given the OK for his sabbatical, I set to work as the family's official travel planner, which included making certain that the minutiae of our home-life – house, dogs, bills - was going to be managed in our absence. And perhaps most uniquely, I drew from my professional expertise as a curriculum designer and educator to develop our kids' study program to meet their school's requirements, while building in the mind-blowing adventures they would soon be having.

So, it was on that day on the banks of the Mekong that I began brainstorming the details of how our family travelled for those glorious months to four continents, twelve countries and a thousand priceless memories. This book is the result.

WHAT'S IN IT FOR YOU?

Throughout the process of writing, I asked myself what information would have made our travel planning easier? Which details from our own experiences on this world tour, plus our many years of global travel as a family, could save other parents hours of time and effort, and help quell worries that come with such an ambitious undertaking?

My expectation is that much of what is written in this book can be adopted by both novice and seasoned family-travellers. Of course, I cannot guarantee that your needs will exactly match those described in these pages, as our family's definition of fun may differ starkly from your own, but I hope it provides you with a solid base from which to begin your unique journey.

LIVING YOUR TRAVEL DREAMS

Have you ever shared your dreams of travel with family or friends only to learn that they have similar desires? This happens to me regularly. It begins with someone mentioning a great adventure or location they may have read about in a magazine or seen on TV. We then move on to exploring the idea further, envisioning how we might adapt it to our kids' interests or a learning opportunity we've longed for. Here are just a few actual conversations I've been part of in recent months:

- *There are cooking classes in Florence that I would love to take.*
- *I've always wanted to spend a few months in Cuba to learn salsa.*
- *I hear you can take yoga classes while trekking in Nepal. That could be tacked onto a trip to India.*
- *If I had the time, I would love to spend a few months in France to practice guitar seriously.*
- *I have a friend who attended a travel writing class in Paris. Her husband and kids explored the city while she was in class. In*

the evenings, they took art classes together in galleries around the city.

- *To improve our Spanish, we're thinking of volunteering at an orphanage in Peru for three months.*
- *I know a couple who cycled from the UK to Holland with their 11-year old son last summer.*

Do any of these ideas appeal to you? Admittedly, they ALL appeal to me! For our family, it has never been a question of which of these brilliant adventures we should have, but rather working out which to do next. Of course, the ideas and options keep rolling in and changing, just as our tastes and interests evolve. As the kids get older, and bolder, we explore options further afield, more foreign. What matters is, with every passing year and new experience under our belts, we see travel ideas less as dreams and more as possibilities.

That's why taking off those months to travel together felt so liberating. We were free to do so many different things, in such a wide variety of locations, from working hands-on to rehabilitate monkeys, collecting wildlife data and tending to a wounded rhino in South Africa, to studying Buddhist chant with a monk in rural Laos and teaching English to children in Zimbabwe. We hiked through New Zealand's lush forests, ate cobra in Vietnam, and learnt to kite surf in the Philippines. We danced with San bush women and attended a Herero tribal wedding in Namibia, and worked on restoring a medieval house in southern France.

In the end, and without exaggeration, we had the most wonderful time of our lives. The coming pages will show you how we did it, and give you plenty of pointers on how you can make your own family's travel dreams reality.

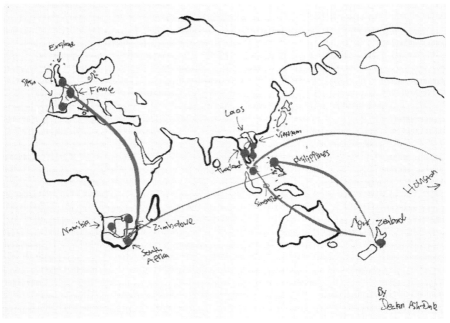

OUR FAMILY'S GAP YEAR ITINERARY

PRE-READING QUESTIONAIRE:

What is your current thinking about taking your family on a gap year adventure? The aim of this book is to gently prod you in that direction, so let's see where you currently stand.

1. *What are the places you dream of seeing, and experiences you imagine having with your family, anywhere in the world? Be bold!*

2. *What would be the ideal length of time for your family gap year tour? Why?*
    (There's nothing magic about 12 months. Your "gap year" could range from a several weeks to years.)

3. *What do you imagine you and your family would get out of a gap year experience? What could it do for you? How might it change each of you?*

4. *Which words describe your current feelings about planning a family gap year experience?*

Excited	*Doubtful*
Overwhelmed	*Expectant*
Nervous	*Ready*
Hopeful	*Something else?*

5. *What do you feel are the greatest obstacles to your family gap year adventure?*

6. *On a scale of one to ten, how ready are you to grab the kids and go?*
    Not ready! 1 2 3 4 5 6 7 8 9 10 *Let's go!*

OBSTACLES THAT STOP FAMILIES FROM TRAVELLING

Despite the scores of people who share the same dreams of exploring the world with their families, few actually follow through. Why is that? What perceived obstacles stand in their ways? I have some theories, developed over years of hearing friends and relatives, quick to tell me that they admire the travel choices we've made for our family, but in the same breath point out their own reasons for never doing it themselves. I think it comes down to a combination of fear, logistics, costs, time and a dread of schooling their children on the road. I'll explore each one in turn.

Fear

Building up the courage to put your current life on hold for an extended period, and take a leap into worlds unfamiliar, is by far the most challenging part of this process, made even more worrisome when you imagine bringing your kids along for the ride.

I have lost count of how many times people have told me that they are frightened to leave their home countries for fear of disease, terrorism, crime or simply not knowing how to function where English is not widely spoken. For even more people, the fear can be sourced back to a general resistance to change. To be sure, knowing that you will always sleep in a comfortable bed, eat familiar food, school your children in a traditional way and interact with people who speak your language, can be very reassuring. But for me, living an entirely static life like that is not unlike hopping from one franchised restaurant to the next, in which you can always be sure of getting the exact same thing every time. It's easier, but it's also limiting the breadth and depth of your life.

Responsible parents, by definition, put their families' safety and well-being ahead of all else, and Sam and I include ourselves in that category. We have never felt that our adventures have put the kids in any greater risk than what we regularly experience on Texas freeways. We're always sure to wear our safety belts, literally and figuratively. We research the locations we plan to visit through the internet, scour books from the *Lonely Planet* series for words of caution and recommendations, seek out travel warnings published by government bodies, and solicit advice from friends (and friends-of-friends) familiar with the country. We work out which airlines are best to fly on, we carry insurance with us and get the recommended immunizations. But we refuse to stay put.

I recall how, just days after the 2005 Bali nightclub bombing, we redirected our vacation plans away from Indonesia to Perth, Australia, where we enjoyed two spontaneous weeks amongst the kangaroos. Similarly, in 2010, just as the Cairo streets began filling with anti-government protestors, we managed to cancel our tour of Egypt in favor of a few weeks in Rome and Sicily. We remained safe, but we didn't stay home.

On my deathbed, will I wish I had spent more of my life working?

Fear can be a logical response. What about those parents who would love nothing more than to live freely with their families for a few months, but worry about keeping their jobs, or their careers, on track? And who could blame them? *Would I have a job to come back to? What impact would an extended absence have on my career?* Only you can answer those questions for yourself. For many toying with the idea of hitting the road with their kids, this worry can be the deal breaker.

For Sam and myself, the issue crept into every early conversation we had about the trip. My husband is a devoted family man, who takes his role as breadwinner seriously. It took time to bring him around to this crazy idea of mine. He needed to weigh the financial risks and the immediate, and long-term, impact it might have on his career. He thought about his current company, his feelings about his job, and the potential market demand for his skills if his company was unwilling to give him a temporary break from work. In time, he deduced that he had developed a strong enough resume over the years to find *a job* when we got back, even if it wasn't *the job*, and that his current position, although a good one, was just *a job*. This decision to take our family around the world was far more than that – it was *our lives*.

For my part, I stuck close to my personal mantra of *I will never regret what I do, I will only regret what I don't do.* Leaning in to these words over the years has served me well. It may have been just a matter of luck, but most of the risks I have taken in the name of adventure over the years have turned out pretty well. I do place a high currency on planning and preparation, which takes some of the uncertainty out of perceived risk. *Unknowables* don't overly intimidate me, and I'm comfortable managing the consequences at the other end.

So, how did it turn out? you ask. For the best. Sam applied for his sabbatical and it was approved. And due to a rather auspicious corporate reorganization, he returned to find a new and improved position waiting for him. *Was this meant to be, or what?*

For me, the gap year gave me the time and space I needed to re-examine what I wanted to do in the next stage of my career, and I came back refreshed, invigorated and ready to get back to work.

So, what about you? If your work situation is what's holding you back, perhaps thinking through your answers to these questions will help bring some clarity.

YOU AS AN EMPLOYEE

- *Over the course of my career, how much would this temporary absence really matter?*
- *When I'm 100 years old, and I look back on my life, what will I think the right decision would have been?*

- *How much do I like my current job? Why?*
- *How much does my current job reflect who I want to be? My values? My life's ambitions?*
- *How might my employer react to my asking for an extended break from work?*
- *Why would my current employer hire me back if I quit?*
- *How would I feel about working for another employer?*
- *What skills, qualifications and experience do I have that another employer would value?*
- *How long would I be willing or able to be without work after the trip?*
- *How would I feel about doing something different when we got back?*
- *How could this be my chance to do that other thing I've been thinking about?*
- *How willing would we be to relocate for my work after the trip?*
- *How might we extend our gap year if another job wasn't immediately available?*
- *What kind of business could I start when we returned?*
- *What are my top five life priorities? To what extent does my current job mesh with these?*

YOU AS A BUSINESS OWNER

- *How could my business continue to run in my absence?*
- *How could I run the business remotely?*
- *In the long run, how would this temporary absence truly matter to my business life?*
- *To what extent do I like what I'm currently doing?*
- *How much does my current business reflect who I want to be? My values? My life's ambitions?*

- *How hard would it be to get the business running again upon my return?*
- *What else could I do when we got back?*
- *What would it mean to work for someone else for a while?*
- *What skills, experience and resources do I have that would enable me to start a new business?*
- *Could I start a business in one of the locations we're planning to visit?*
- *How might we extend our gap year if we had the freedom to choose?*
- *What are my top five life priorities? How do these match with my current business?*

Ultimately, the choice is yours. Will your life be defined by your courage or your fears?

Logistics

"It would be way too difficult. And I wouldn't know where to be begin..." are sentiments shared by many parents who baulk at the thought of making their travel desires reality. Indeed, there are hurdles to overcome to take your family on the road for an extended period. Here are just a few you might need to navigate through, which will be addressed in the coming pages:

Before the trip:

- *Who will take care of our house and pets?*
- *What administrative details, like taxes and bills, will we need to get sorted?*
- *How can we reduce our travel costs?*

During the trip

- *Where will we go and what will we do?*
- *How will we educate the kids on the road?*

After the trip:

- *How will the experience change us?*
- *How can we make this experience stick with us for years to come?*

The following pages provide advice about how to tackle these issues, and many more. The most important message I hope you take away from this is *keep your eye on the prize!* No problem is so great that it should stop you from fulfilling your lifelong desires. Trust me on this! Those extraordinary months of exploring the world with our children have been the highlight of our time together so far. We will spend the rest of our days cherishing those memories we created together, and the benefits to each of us individually, to our marriage and to our family, cannot be overstated.

Cost

There is no doubt that money is a genuine hurdle that stops families from travelling. As everyone's circumstances are different, I am not about to delve deeply into the intricacies of how to increase incomes and reduce costs to travel, although I will offer a few cost-saving tips and tricks along the way.

What I do recommend is that you have a serious think about where your money currently goes every month. How much do you spend on eating out or on random clothes shopping? Do you pay for cable and internet? What about monthly gym memberships fees, parking and gas costs? Do you pay for your child's tuition? How much do you spend on coffee every week? What else do you spend your money on that would not be the case if you were traveling?

If you're coming from a country where the currency is strong and the cost of living is relatively high, you could find countless idyllic destinations around the world where your money goes much further. In fact, there is a real possibility that your monthly expenses could be lower, perhaps much lower, while you're travelling than while you're at home. *It's true!*

Most of the countries we visited during our gap year can be inexpensive to travel in if you make the right choices. The US dollar goes a long way in Vietnam, Laos, the Philippines, South Africa and Namibia. New Zealand and Singapore were our most expensive destinations, followed by France. Zimbabwe, despite its crippled economy, is not an inexpensive travel option, unless you make choices like we did to volunteer rather than stay at a high-end resort. For these reasons, our average monthly expenses were less than they were at home.

It all comes down to selecting what works best for you. What do you want to see? What do you want to do? How do you want to do and see it? Each answer comes with its own price tag.

Many of the most well-travelled people I know have chosen to live differently than other people do, often on considerably less money. In general, these people have chosen to place less value on possessions and more on experiences.

Our final itinerary was a compromise between our desires and what we felt we could afford. When we made choices in favor of saving money, we rarely did so thinking that we were accepting something less. Extensive international travel has taught us that experiences that cost little can be the most precious. Spending the day looking for shells on a beach in Goa with the children of a local fisherman costs nothing, but the memory can be priceless. Taking a guided multi-city group tour through Europe can be expensive, and can leave one feeling bored and frustrated. I have no doubt that had we stayed in

5-star accommodation throughout the tour, visited only luxurious safari lodges in Africa, and eaten at the finest restaurants in every location, we would not have had such a wonderful time. In fact, I am certain of it!

To be sure, we could have paid less for our family gap year. We could have foregone the camper van in New Zealand, and stayed at a discount hotel in Singapore. In these instances, and some others, we chose to splurge. That's what the process of itinerary planning is all about – it's a series of choices, and each has its own cost. (Coming chapters examine family travel options for a range of budgets.)

Over the years, I have met a great many teachers who have covered the globe on a budget. One dear friend, Shannon, a teacher from Vancouver, trekked in Nepal with a Sherpa guide for several weeks. Not long after, she travelled by van across Africa from Nairobi to London. Another summer she trekked in Peru and the following year through the Swiss Alps with groups of friends. These amazing adventures were all done on a teacher's salary.

Sam and I lived in Asia for several years and during that time we met many expat teachers, couples with children who spent their winter, spring and summer vacations backpacking through Sri Lanka, volunteering in India, lazing on a beach in Thailand and exploring the grasslands of Mongolia. These families chose to reserve a greater percentage of their income for travel, by settling for somewhat smaller accommodation or foregoing a car for public transportation. This group saw this as a small price to pay for a life of *regular newness* and exotic locations whenever school was let out. In the name of freedom and adventure, they made choices that people in higher-income brackets are sometimes less willing to make.

My brother, Michael, makes his living editing academic science papers through a company he set up in Taiwan. He doesn't actually live in Taiwan. He doesn't live anywhere, in fact. But he lives everywhere.

When he is not sitting in cafes around the globe working on papers, he is climbing Himalayan mountains, motorcycling through Turkey, skiing in Canada, studying Chinese in Beijing or taking stunning photos of churches in Armenia. He is an avid travel photographer, a Canadian-champion karate expert who earned his black-belt in Japan, and recently designed and built himself a stunning house with a spectacular view on a remote Philippine island. He is a genuine global vagabond who lives on a shoestring, but has had adventures beyond most people's wildest imaginations. Admittedly, he is doing this largely on his own, without kids in tow, but I am not convinced that it's the only way such a life can be lived.

Giorgio is a single father who lives between Austria, Israel and the Philippines. His income comes from rooms he rents through *Airbnb*, and a beach-side kite surfing school he set up in Boracay, Philippines. He homeschools his two primary-school-aged daughters, with whom he recently completed two ambitious driving tours; one through Russia, and the other through Southern Africa. He sees no reason to give up his unconventional lifestyle while his girls are enjoying such quality time with their father and seeing the world in the process.

What we have learnt over the years is that there are countless ways to finance global travel. Some people choose to save for months or years in advance to go on that one dream holiday, while others build a permanent travel budget into their monthly expenses to enjoy regular, shorter trips. More and more people we meet earn money while on the road, by writing articles, working through internet-related businesses or renting out rooms back home. An Australian hairdresser I know, sailed around the world with her family for two years, largely financed by doing the hair of other sailors at the marinas where they docked. And I work with my executive coaching clients over the telephone and Skype, allowing me the freedom to work from anywhere.

Of course, long-term travel becomes more feasible for those of us on a budget by reducing costs. Flights, accommodation, meals and overland travel are the overheads that can make travel prohibitively expensive for many people. Throughout the coming pages, I point out ways to reduce some of these costs.

Time

"I don't have the time."

"I could never take that much time off work."

"This just isn't the right time."

Oh, the number of times I have heard people say these words – people who dream of travelling the world with their children, but doubt they could ever make it happen because they are convinced they have no time.

Do you say these things to yourself? Have you ever considered how much more constructive it might be to say:

"Let's consider our options."

"Let's think creatively about how we can make this happen."

"I'll simply make the time."

"If not now, when?"

One rainy Sunday in Houston, while the kids were busily working their ways through stacks of middle school homework in the dining room, Sam and I had a chance to talk. I had just finished reading *The 4 Hour Workweek*, by Tim Ferris, recommended by a perceptive friend. It was the right book for me at the right time. It puts forth a convincing argument that the world is filled with diverse and fascinating things to do and learn, and we should make the most of it.

The reason why Ferris' book struck a chord with me at that time was that we had reached a bit of a low point in our family life. I had given up a stimulating life I had built for myself in Asia to relocate for Sam's work, and had not yet managed to feel settled. Sam wasn't particularly enjoying his new role, and the kids were being sucked dry by a homework-driven school system. Ferris' book reminded us that there are other ways to live!

Sam and I talked. He then read the book. We talked some more. And then we asked ourselves, *If not now, when?* At 12 and 13, the kids were the ideal ages to go on the type of journey Sam and I craved. They were old enough to participate in more challenging adventure travel than they had been previously, and to fully grasp and remember what they were seeing. This was key for us because although the kids had been to a great many places already, we noticed that a lot of the details were missed or being forgotten with each passing year. They were finally old enough to be impressed by cultural differences and to take note of the historical, political and economic features of each location we visited, which had always been important to Sam and me. Moreover, Declan was one-year shy of entering high school, when the challenges of taking him out of school would have increased exponentially.

We spent the next three or four months playing with the idea of an extended world tour and bouncing it off our community of well-travelled friends and family. In time, we found ourselves splitting our spare downtime between thinking about what form our adventure might take, and how we might make it happen. By the end, our desire to go far outweighed the fears and pressures to stay put. When Sam finally broached the subject of a sabbatical with his company, we had already decided that if they said no he would quit, and the consequences would be dealt with later. In the end, his sabbatical was approved, and four months later we were boarding the first of our 15 flights around the world.

Now, back to you. The length and design of your family's journey depends on your circumstances and priorities. The concept of a *gap year* should not to be taken literally. There is nothing magical about 12 months. Some lucky few stretch their journeys over multiple years, whereas others manage to enjoy meaningful adventures covering several glorious weeks. However long you can wrangle, I say *think BIG* - if not in the length of time you can get away, then in the magnitude of your life-changing experiences.

There is never a perfect time, and waiting and overthinking only increases the chances of your never going. Instead, think to yourself *The kids won't be with us forever. If not now, when?* And what about in years to come, looking back at those precious years with your kids? Would you rather be saying to yourself *We should have!* or *We did it!?*

Schooling on the road

There is no doubt that the thought of schooling your own child can be a daunting one for any parent, particularly so if you are planning to do it while travelling. Questions begin to plague your mind like:

- *What curriculum should I teach?*
- *How can studying get done while we are busy travelling?*
- *Will the school allow us to take our child out temporarily?*
- *Will my child be able to keep up in class when it's time to return to school?*
- *Will my child learn enough to make it worthwhile?*

Firstly, you'll need to work out if your child needs to move into her next grade when she returns, or if you are happy with her staying in her current grade. If you choose the latter, then there is unlikely to be specific progress markers to aim toward, so you will be free to educate your child as you wish.

If you are like us, however, and decide that you would like your child to advance to his next grade level after your gap year, then you will need a plan. You may decide to rely entirely on pre-designed homeschooling curricula offered by an academic institution, an online educational service or your local school board. Alternatively, you may do as we did, and design your own program to match, and even enhance, your travel adventures. *Why be required to read about the American Revolution while we're camping in the Kalahari Desert? Wouldn't studying the San Bush people be more relevant?*

I drew from my years as a curriculum designer and educator to develop assignments that helped our kids learn about the places we were visiting. Twelve-year old Scout, for instance, produced an essay on efforts to protect a coral reef off of a small Philippine island we were staying on, based on interviews with local fishermen and concerned business owners. In South Africa, fourteen-year old Declan researched rhino poaching in Limpopo, including interviews with the head of a rhino protection organization and a leader of an anti-poaching squad. In Laos, both children enjoyed writing fictional accounts of life as a Buddhist monk, drawing from what they had learnt through fascinating conversations with a senior monk. These are just a few examples of their eye-opening projects.

Downtimes were spent devouring more fiction and non-fiction books than the kids could ever have managed during a regular school year. They completed a school year's-worth of math in a fraction of the time. Declan explored science topics which had long interested him, from black holes to solar energy to contagious diseases. We took advantage of being in New Zealand, where evidence of seismic activity is prevalent, to teach Scout physical geography topics that she would be missing due to her absence from school. Aspects of meteorology – weather and currents – were covered as we traveled through multiple climates. And in Africa, the kids' attention was focused on wildlife behavior and conservation.

In truth, schooling on the road made our family gap year far richer than had we been on a traditional family vacation. Every family member was more present, observant and conscious of what we were seeing and experiencing. To top it off, the kids returned home relaxed, recharged and entirely prepared to re-enter school at their next grade levels.

If you would like to know more about how we schooled our kids on the road, I provide a detailed account in the second book of this series, *Schooling-Through-Travel: How the World Became our Kids' Classroom*. I provide descriptions of our teaching methods, examples of specific assignments, materials and teaching supplies we brought along, and how we communicated the kids' learning back to their school. I also added information on how to adapt the approach to different age groups.

Bear with me, schooling on the road is not as scary as it sounds. In fact, it may turn out, as it did for us, to be one of the most rewarding things you will ever do as a parent.

5 TAKE-AWAYS

1. **Fear** – Don't give your fears the power to stop you from living your dreams. Do your research, talk to others who have done what you imagine doing, read travel stories, and assess your life's priorities.

2. **Logistics** - Make a plan. Progress at a steady pace. Ask for help and advice, and utilize the wide range of information sources available to travelling families online and in this book. Don't allow the many details of your family gap year to overwhelm you.

3. **Costs** - Don't assume that your expenses on the road will be greater than your monthly expenses back home. The cost of your family gap year is a matter of choice. Explore your options before determining your budget.

4. **Time** - *If not now, when?*

5. **Schooling** – Your child has the potential to learn more on the road than she ever could sitting in a classroom, particularly if you focus her attention on the places you are at each moment. *Observe, listen, experience, connect and seek to understand the wonderful world around you!*

PART A
VISION

Chapter 2:
Defining your Family's Gap Year

One question I am regularly asked is *How did you ever come up with that itinerary?* Admittedly, we covered a lot of territory during our family gap year and did an amazing range of interesting and unexpected things. Our family appreciates less-conventional travel, is willing to do so on a shoestring, and accept all that that entails. Sam and I have traveled the world with our kids since they were babies, choosing destinations that could appeal to a range of tastes. Even if the travel choices described in the coming pages would not be yours, my hope is that these anecdotes still inspire you to just grab the kids and go... somewhere!

WORKING OUT YOUR GOALS

Before you begin working out the specifics of your family gap year itinerary, I suggest that you and your family come to an agreement on your general goals. Begin with the end in mind by asking yourselves - *Ultimately, what do we most want to get out of this experience? Are we after relaxation, adventure or growth? Or something else?*

Your answer should determine the itinerary you design. If you dream of experiencing new cultures while exploring the great outdoors, then perhaps forego that return visit to Colorado this time and give Nepal, Peru or the French Pyrenees a try. If relaxation is a high priority for you, then perhaps a multi-stop European vacation should be postponed in favor of a few weeks in a rented house in Tuscany. (This may not be as expensive as it sounds, by the way. See Chapter 8: *Where to Stay.*)

For our family, the answer to this question was a combination of relaxation, adventure and growth. Tim Ferris hit a chord with me in his book, *The 4-Hour Work Week,* when he narrowed his life's guiding principles down to three simple but essential ones - *To love, to be loved and to learn.* Indeed, without even articulating it to myself, those values had driven most of my life's choices and influenced our decision to temporarily put *normal* life on hold to explore the world together.

Sam and I wanted those months to be about focusing in on our family, allowing each one of us to discover new passions, and to grow from what we collectively saw and experienced. This was finally our chance to raise the kids exactly as we had always dreamed of – exposing them to exotic lands and diverse peoples, spending hours talking and laughing amongst ourselves and sharing what we were learning together.

Ah, the romance of spontaneous travel!

When I first began travelling as a young adult, before the internet was even a thing, venturing to places with nothing more than a worn copy of *Lonely Planet* meant that spontaneity was guaranteed. I might have had a vague idea of what I was going to find, but was far more likely to show up at a place and only then begin looking for accommodation. I would arrive largely unaware of any recommended restaurants, desirable neighborhoods or local foods to try. I simply took it in my stride and liked it that way!

A few years later, before we were engaged, Sam and I spontaneously hopped onto a plane of Indonesia's discount airline, *Merpati,* to spend a few days discovering Sumatra. We found that this airline, which has since mercifully been closed down, included seats that leaned forward in *the crash position* unless forcibly pushed upright. The cockpit door flapped open throughout the flight forcing us to view our baby-faced pilot bouncing through the turbulence. The most memorable feature was the attendant call button that, when pressed by any passenger for any reason, set off a piercing screech so alarming that we, and every other inexperienced Merpati passenger, felt compelled to return our seats to the crash position.

Beyond that terrifying flight, however, the rest of the trip was a blur of wacky, unpredictable and highly memorable experiences. We drove through the rainy - *Oh, it's monsoon season? How about that!* - countryside on the back of a rusty Honda motorbike, cloaked in two enormous yellow rain ponchos purchased for less than a dollar at a local night market. We explored villages, haggled with weavers, and were crushed between tiny ladies on local buses who carried baskets of fruit and poultry - dead and alive. None of it was planned. None of it was particularly comfortable. And certainly, none of it was expected. But it was one of the best adventures of our lives.

Why did I tell you this story? Because I want to warn you against over-planning your trip, since the unexpected can be even more special and memorable than the planned. That said, it is undoubtedly more difficult for families. Single travelers can make choices according to their whims. Couples may be slightly more bound to planning if their tastes and interests are not entirely in accord. For families, even more opinions come into the equation, kids can have different needs, perhaps a greater preference for common comforts and, as responsible parents, you know they need to be kept safe. Ever since we had the kids we have not once (OK, maybe once!) put our lives at risk on the back of beaten motorcycles, weaving through undisciplined third-world traffic. But we haven't forgotten that the willingness to turn on a dime when an appealing opportunity presents itself is one of the best attitudes to travel with. So, as you design your family's itinerary, consider leaving room for some spontaneity.

Over-planning vs. under-planning

As part of the researching and planning processes, it's important to establish to what extent your tour needs to be determined in advance, and how much flexibility can be built in. One family may dream of pointing their sailboat in a general direction, allowing the currents and winds to ultimately determine which Caribbean ports they reach *en route*. Others may choose to follow a specific path through the key tourist destinations of central India, dictated by set dates, booked guides and confirmed hotel rooms from beginning to end. Where do you suspect your family sits on this spectrum?

Our family managed to visit a total of 12 countries during our gap year, following a pre-determined around-the-world flight schedule. We left the regional flights largely open, allowing for some measure of spontaneous decision-making along the way. For instance, out of Singapore we were free to choose and change our next destinations within South-East Asia – we ultimately decided upon Vietnam, Thailand, Laos and the Philippines. From Johannesburg, our destinations and timing in Africa were, to some degree, flexible, so from South Africa we elected to head for Namibia and then to Zimbabwe.

What about your family? Ask yourselves *How tightly do we need to stick to a specific pre-planned itinerary and schedule?* To help answer this question, consider issues that have impacted our decisions over the years:

Pros of pre-planning/pre-booking your itinerary:

- Enjoying the sense of comfort that comes with knowing what's in store.

- Avoiding using precious travel time to work out further arrangements. (Take it from me, trying to make bookings without reliable telephone or internet access can be problematic and time consuming.)

- Securing better deals on flights and accommodation.
- Improving your chances of getting into popular sites, particularly during high tourist seasons.
- Knowing which clothing, immunizations and other things (sleeping bags, flashlights, toiletries, etc.) you might need for specific locations.

Pros for keeping your itinerary flexible:

- Being open to opportunities that present themselves along the way.
- Making choices about what to do next based on how you're feeling at the time.
- Getting better deals on flights and accommodation. (Yes, sometimes you can find great deals closer to the time you need them.)
- Having the freedom to adapt locations and activities to weather or other local conditions.
- Developing a genuine confidence in your ability to handle any eventuality on the spot. (I personally feel that this is one of the greatest benefits of casual travel.)

TIP

Before confirming any reservations, be it for flights, accommodation, activities or transportation, determine your ability to cancel or make changes, and what penalties you will incur.

Be clear on what your cancellation insurance covers, and what is required to get reimbursed, such as receipts and airline tickets.

Although this is by no means a rule, I have observed that experienced travellers appear more comfortable with leaving space in their itineraries for spontaneous detours. That certainly applies to our family. With each new journey abroad, we become increasingly comfortable waking up not knowing what the day has in store for us, nor where we will sleep that night. *What a wonderfully liberating feeling!*

> *"Well, we were planning on staying at Etosha National Park one more night, but we now have a chance to meet a community of San people. When will we ever get such a chance again? We have a reservation at the park but I'm happy to forego the deposit if they won't give us a refund."*
>
> *Actual conversation*

Skimming vs. diving

Do we want to skim through many different places or dive in and explore one or just a few locations in depth?

As your family's tour planner, consider where you want to perch on the balance between what I call *skimming* and *diving* approaches to travel. Some families embark on their gap year tours purely to get away from it all, to detox from the stress of their regular lives and to build more peaceful relationships with each other. For them, an eclectic itinerary like ours might not be suitable. They might choose instead to spend their entire time sailing between ports in the Mediterranean, or to narrow in on one or two locations, such as a campsite on the Canadian West Coast, on a beach in Thailand or in a village in Croatia where they can live as the local people do, learn to cook the cuisine, practice the language or simply to chill.

Over the years we have covered the gambit between skimming and diving. On our honeymoon, Sam and I took six weeks to drive through seven European countries. We spent two or three days in each major city *en route*, visited the requisite museums, castles and opera houses. We ate the celebrated dishes in each location, and drove away from each proudly claiming *We have been there!* In retrospect, we just skimmed the surface, having missed so much of what each place had to offer. Of course, we still had a brilliant time!

We have also done it the other way. Over the years, as a couple and then as a family, we have accumulated months of living in one quaint village in France. We know the local grocer and restaurateurs, have developed friendships with villagers (and their dogs), and are sure to visit the same outdoor markets every Saturday and Sunday morning. In our hearts, for a short time every year, we are French locals. To be sure, it has been a luxury to spend so much quality time in one place, but there's always that nagging feeling that *Next time we should explore more of the region.*

Liberté en France.

There is no best way to travel. If this will be your one chance to visit a place with your kids, perhaps skimming to see all the major sites in the region is the way to go. On the other hand, you may hold tightly to a dream of living like an Italian for a few months, or learning a special skill or participating in an activity – cooking, dancing, painting, climbing, skiing, kayaking, yoga, language study – that would require a commitment of time in one location, and thus diving.

Our family's gap year sat somewhere in the middle of this spectrum. Since the kids had just entered their teens, we could not help but feel that our time horizon with them was growing shorter and shorter. There was a list of things we wanted to do and see as a family before they grew up and flew the nest. On the other hand, we did not want to feel that the whole adventure was a mad dash from one place to the next, never having the time to soak anything in. Once again, we included two months diving in our French village, but we also skimmed through places, like Namibia and New Zealand, where there was so much we wanted to see.

Diving in Vietnam

A small hamlet outside of Can Tho, Vietnam, turned out to be one place where we stayed put and dove for a few weeks rather than skimming through the country south to north as originally planned.

There is much to see in Vietnam, as Sam and I discovered before having kids. We had explored the country just as the US began re-establishing ties with that country. In fact, in November 2000, we landed on the Hanoi airport tarmac to find Air Force One waiting for President Bill Clinton to conclude his historic summit with the Communist regime.

Remnants of the Cold War years were still very much in evidence back then. Tourism was in its infancy. Sam and I explored hill tribe villages on the back of a weather-beaten Russian Minsk motorcycle. Younger locals, dressed in traditional garb, assumed we were Russian, while the elderly spoke with us in broken French, a leftover from the pre-Communist colonial period. Few people we met along the way even attempted English. It was a wonderfully foreign experience.

By the time we arrived in Saigon with the children 16 years later, however, it was clear that the economic opening of Vietnam had brought with it an overgrowth of franchised eateries and brand names. The international language was now widely spoken. The city's air was filled with dust and noise, as the charming pedal-driven rickshaws had long been replaced by cars, motorcycles and tour buses. There was a new frenetic pace, a general look and feel that made it largely indistinguishable from dozens of other South-East Asian cities we had visited over the years. It was a bit more of a struggle to find what was quintessentially Vietnamese.

Rather than risking the disappointment of not finding the Vietnam we remembered, Sam and I made a quick decision to cancel our plans for an overland tour, and instead settle down in huts on the edge of the Mekong Delta - the perfect antidote to the chaos we had found in the cities. Our days were spent close to the delta banks, cycling along palm-shaded pathways between quiet villages, feasting on sweet mangos and pineapples from the floating wholesale water-market, observing traditional trades like noodle making, rice trading and fishing, and even giving crocodile and cobra a taste.

This slow and gentle time together was rich and entirely satisfying. None of us felt that we had missed out by not covering the country to the extent we had originally planned. Quite the contrary.

BANANA PALMS AND NON LA HATS PROTECTED US FROM THE SUN.
MEKONG DELTA, VIETNAM.

Diving in Laos

One of our more thrilling plans for Laos included zip-lining through gibbon-inhabited rainforests along the Thai border to treehouses built high above the treeline. The reservations were made in advance, and the two-day river boat ride up to the Thai border had been organized, only to have our plans dashed when we landed in Luang Prabang. The region had been hit by the worst cold spell in living memory. Rumor had it that snow had fallen at higher elevations. Along the streets people crowded around coal fires built in small clay pots normally reserved for cooking. We were of the lucky few housed with something resembling a heater. (Buildings in Luang Prabang, a lovely UNESCO protected heritage town, were not intended to keep out freezing temperatures.) We had not packed for those conditions

- our cotton shorts and t-shirts were entirely unsuitable for the cold weather that had enveloped the region right up to central China. Without a doubt, visiting the gibbons under those circumstances would have been miserable.

With little other choice, we reluctantly cancelled our reservations and began scouring online travel sites and our handy *Lonely Planet* guide to work out how best to spend the next few days. We found a variety of cultural activities that allowed us to stay warm-ish and dry-ish until the sun finally returned to thaw our bones. We took a fascinating tour of local vegetable and meat markets, enjoyed a day-long cooking class including recipes on how to use local barks and grasses. *Delicious!* Scout and I took a class in traditional weaving led by a Hmong tribeswoman who took the opportunity to educate us about courtship practices, wedding rituals and family life within Laos' mountain tribes.

Once the weather improved, we ventured out beyond Luang Prabang to traditional villages and Buddhist temples hours up-river. They were well worth the wait!

It was not exactly the tour of Laos we had planned, but by being flexible and relaxed we managed to turn a disappointment into another kind of special.

Skimming in New Zealand

New Zealand was a country we skimmed through, primarily because we had set aside only four weeks to see a list of sites Sam had long wanted to introduce us to. There is so much to see and do throughout his native country. We travelled by camper van to explore numerous natural wonders between the Coromandel Peninsula on the North Island and mid-way down the South Island. We hiked, white-water rafted, sea kayaked, caved and stuffed ourselves with New Zealand's famous meat pies.

Our hectic pace needed to be adapted to the kids' energy levels, making sure that we did not exceed four hours on the road at a time, unless absolutely necessary. This lesson served us well later in Namibia, where we once again covered a considerable distance by road.

The visit to New Zealand was a great success, but it took a lot out of us, particularly Sam who drove the camper van for the entirety of the tour. By the time we reached the Philippines, we were reconsidering our ambitious plans for the coming month.

Downtime in the Philippines

Even when you're having the time of your life, travel can be exhausting. Make sure to pepper your itinerary with periods purely for rest and relaxation, particularly if you are travelling with kids who can get tired and bored more easily.

Our original plan was to enjoy the sun and surf of the Philippines for just a few days before heading off to explore either the cultural sites of Myanmar or to enjoy a unique yoga-trek out of Pokhara, Nepal. It turned out, however, that our driving marathon in New Zealand had taken its toll and our ambitious plans for Nepal and Myanmar started to sound like a bit too much work. To give either destination its due attention would have required more time and energy than we had. So, we put them both on our family's *Next Time* shelf, and moved into a couple of huts on a secluded stretch of beach on a remote Philippine island. *Tropical paradise for just dollars a day!* It gave us plenty of time to sunbath, swim, meditate, read, snorkel, study, befriend local people . . . and eat our weights in mangos.

OUR DESERTED ISLAND PARADISE
TABLAS, PHILIPPINES

5 TAKE-AWAYS

1. Agree as a family what your ultimate gap year goal is – adventure, relaxation, education, visiting family or a mix.

2. Decide how comfortable you and your family are with spontaneous travel versus plans clearly set in advance.

3. If a great opportunity presents itself during your travels, know in advance what the penalties would be for changing or cancelling your reservations.

4. Work out which locations you are willing to skim through, and which you would prefer to dive in and explore in depth.

5. Factor downtime into your itinerary.

Chapter 3
Family Travel Ideas

I hope the ideas that follow open you to options beyond your standard travel path. It is not, of course, an exhaustive list of the amazing adventures available to travelling families today, but it might get you thinking about a greater range possibilities.

> **Note to the reader:**
>
> *Throughout this book, I refer to websites I found helpful in preparing for our family's gap year. I suggest, however, that you do not stick exclusively to these. Every day, new and improved travel websites are being launched. Researching what's out there is part of the fun.*

PATCHWORK HOLIDAY

For your family gap year, you may be imagining spending the entirety of your vacation renting a house at the base of the Swiss Alps, where you could live as the locals do, hiking and breathing in the clean mountain air, perhaps eating stacks of chocolate, and learning how to make a really great cheese fondue.

Or, you may choose as Elizabeth Gilbert describes her memoir, *Eat Pray, Love,* three different places to soak in – in her case, Italy, India and Bali – neatly divided over 12 months.

Our family gap year may best be described as a patchwork holiday, where experiences of varied qualities and lengths were sewn together over several glorious months. Our journey covered a wide spectrum - French countryside, African *bushveld*, Buddhist monasteries, lush rainforests, tropical beaches, monkey cages, barren deserts, European cathedrals and a South-East Asian delta. Each experience was a holiday unto itself.

As you read through the following travel ideas, think about whether you're a solid pattern or a patchwork kind of family.

HISTORICAL & CULTURAL TOURS

Our gap year included tours of museums, religious and historic sites, as well as exchanges with diverse cultures on four distinct continents. At 12 and 13-turned-14, our kids were finally old enough to grasp much of the significance of what they were experiencing. That was less so the case when they were younger.

FUN FACTS

My friend, Tina, who has travelled extensively with her children all over the world explains *"when kids have heard about places through movies, books or games, they get excited when they see the real thing.*

Prepare yourself with fun facts about your destination that will entertain the kids while you're there – funny, historical, geographical and cultural facts. Play games, read books and watch kids' movies related to your destination before and during the trip, and on the flight.

Before going to England and Scotland, our son re-read all of the Harry Potter books and our toddler read Paddington books. We watched the movie "The Water Horse" to get the feel for the Loch Ness monster and we played the British version of Monopoly. I also got our older son to watch some historical movies."

Back when Declan was ten and Scout was eight we went to Italy, England and Scotland. Our aim was to explore historic sites and museums, as well as some of the world's finest art galleries. But given their ages, how much did they genuinely get out of those experiences? Sam and I are avid history enthusiasts and we spent a great deal of time telling the kids animated stories about what we were seeing, to bring the history alive in their minds. Some of it stuck, to be sure, but if we were to ask them about those trips now they might be limited to faint recollections of the delicious gelato they ate at the foot of the Spanish Steps in Rome, the sheep they played with in the Scottish Highlands and the thrill of navigating through London's Tube network. Is that enough to make such a trip worthwhile? Could be.

Parents need to be realistic about what they want their children to get out of the places they visit. *Is this the right time to take our kids to that location, or should we wait a few years?* For us, in the early years, the mere experience of travelling, of being exposed to different sights and smells, tastes and sensations, was what it was all about, even when the children were unlikely to remember many of the specifics.

When the kids were just four and five years old we took them to Siam Reap, Cambodia to deliver hygiene and educational supplies to local schools. As part of the trip we got up before 4:00a.m. to watch the sunrise over Angkor Wat. It was a spectacular sight for Sam and me, but the little ones, unsurprisingly, failed to see the point. There was plenty of whining before they fell asleep in our arms just as the sun rose. To this day our kids fondly remember the hours spent playing with the Cambodian children at the schools we visited, but nothing about exploring one of the Wonders of the World.

KIDS KNOW THAT THE INTERNATIONAL LANGUAGE IS ACTUALLY A SMILE AND A GIGGLE.
SIAM REAP, CAMBODIA

Should we have held off on that trip until the kids were older, so they could remember it today? My answer is no, and I try to justify it this way - each international experience brings them closer to *feeling* part of a greater world, where things are always changing, not always comfortable, but where differences are accepted, expected and appreciated.

Just watch as your child gradually shows a higher degree of self-confidence as she encounters different cultures, attempts to make herself understood where her language is not spoken, eats foods she's never seen before, and accepts that *in this place, I'm the different one.* These kinds of kids scan maps like others might magazines or picture books. They see the world as a place to explore, not to be afraid of.

Helpful Hint

The Horrible Histories video series is a genuinely entertaining source of information about European (as well as Egyptian and Incan) history. Our CD collection travels with us while touring Europe, as we all enjoy watching them after long days of exploring. Some of the Horrible Histories clips can be found on YouTube.

KIDS THE WORLD OVER ENJOY AN OREO.
LAOS

Our family gap year revealed how firmly the kids had reached the age when they could learn specific details of what they were experiencing, in ways that would stick with them for the rest of their lives. Now, our kids can cook Lao dishes out of various barks and grasses, distinguish wildlife footprints in the South African bush, use basic phrases in a handful of languages, make a bow and arrow as the San Bush People of the Kalahari taught them to, handle themselves in a cage full of semi-wild vervet monkeys, navigate through the delicious tapestry of a French village market, amongst many, many other things.

DECLAN LEARNING TO RAIN DANCE, SAN BUSHMAN STYLE.
NAMIBIA

BEACH HOLIDAYS

Lazing on a beach, drinking coconut cocktails while enjoying occasional dips in crystal clear water can make for a wonderful holiday, and is suitable for any age group. Another definite advantage is that they can be some of the least expensive holiday options out there, if you choose your location and accommodation wisely.

Declan was 4-months old when we took him on his first beach-resort holiday, and Scout was only 11-weeks old on her first one. In both cases, we went to Bali, Indonesia. It was relaxing, comfortable and reasonably priced. We were living in Singapore at the time, conveniently located near a variety of beach resort locations in Malaysia, Thailand, Philippines, Indonesia and even Australia.

During our gap year, we wanted to soak up some tropical sun and chose the Philippines because of its well-known kite-surfing destination, Boracay. After completing a round of surfing lessons, our family took a two-hour boat ride to Tablas Island, where we enjoyed weeks of slow living in modest huts on a deserted white beach, facing directly onto what felt like our very own coral reef. Our mornings and evenings were spent snorkeling and meditating on the beach, while the hot afternoons were spent reading, writing and working through homeschooling assignments. It was the perfect place to detox from our stressful lives in the US, and we easily could have stayed on for months longer had it not been for our long, ambitious list of other things to do and places to visit.

Aside from the cost of kite surfing lessons, our time in the Philippines was inexpensive. Even if living in simple beachside huts is not your thing, reasonably priced resorts can be found throughout South-East Asia, and many with facilities ideal for families, like swimming pools, children's activity centers, play groups, and even babysitters. No doubt similar experiences can be enjoyed in the Caribbean, Mediterranean, Central and South America, Sri Lanka and India, amongst other places.

It can sometimes be easier to find accommodation gems once on the ground, so consider booking a hotel or apartment for your first three or four days, during which time you can seek out local advice on options off the beaten track. This advice works best during off-peak seasons when places are less likely to be fully booked. For high-seasons, your best bet is to book your entire stay in advance. (For more on planning your accommodations, see Chapter 8: *Where to Stay.*)

To pre-empt a common question about beach holidays in developing countries, we have never been affected by health or safety worries. We apply mosquito repellent when necessary, eat at reputable restaurants, take care to drink plenty of bottled water and follow common sense behaviors when out on the streets. The only scare we have ever had was when 10-year old Declan got severely dehydrated in Bali after too much time bodysurfing in the blazing sun, but that could have happened anywhere.

DECLAN & SCOUT ENJOYING PERFECT BEACHSIDE FUN WITH THEIR NEW FOREVER-FRIENDS CHERYL-ANN, ANGEL, ROMER AND MABEL.
PHILIPPINES

Of course, it is always wise to have proper medical insurance and to keep emergency numbers close at hand. We have also been careful to keep our immunizations up-to-date and top up with ones recommended for specific areas we plan to visit. (See Chapter 9: *Pack Your Bags* to learn what we know about immunizations.)

CAMPER VAN/RV TRAVEL

Many of the pros and cons of camper travel were learnt on our tour through New Zealand. In retrospect, it was a fun way to see the country and I am glad we gave it a try. The campsites we found were, for the most part, nice and well-equipped, including swimming pools, convenience stores, as well as laundry and cooking facilities. Most importantly, they brought us close to the beautiful country we had come to see.

I can certainly imagine it being an ideal way to travel for a family with smaller children who have a lot of luggage to haul around and would enjoy the extra personal space in their vehicle. I cannot, however, imagine choosing to travel this way again now that the kids are well into their teens and our son is teetering on 6'2" in height. By the end of the tour, we were feeling rather claustrophobic and starting to get on each other's nerves. The hassle of having to pack everything up each morning just to walk around inside the vehicle began to wear, as did having to store everything away to drive.

That said, several of our friends have spent their entire family gap years travelling around North America and Australia in the comfort and convenience of RVs, so I would certainly not rule it out as an appealing option.

Here are some questions to ask yourself before adding a camper experience to your itinerary:

- *How big does the camper need to be to accommodate our family comfortably?*
- *How much will it actually cost, including insurance, fuel, campsite and possibly ferry fees? Note that some of these costs may be offset by cooking meals rather than dining out.*
- *How does the cost compare with the average cost of hotels/B&Bs in the locations we will be visiting?*
- *Are campsites readily available on the route we are planning?*
- *Do the campsites include electricity and water hook-ups for campers?*
- *What other facilities do we require, or would enjoy, in a campsite?*

- *Are the campsites within easy reach of the places we want to visit?*

- *If we don't rent a camper, how will we travel around? By car? Train? Bus? How much will that cost?*

- *Would we be satisfied simply sleeping in a tent? Or, would we be happy to sleep in a tent occasionally, and at a hotel/B&B other nights? How might that affect costs?*

- *Which side of the road do they drive on in that country – left or right? Are we comfortable with that?*

TENT CAMPING

Into the wild

Wilderness camping with kids is an affordable and popular family travel option, especially in places like the US, Canada, New Zealand and Northern and Western Europe. Today's tents come in a such a wide variety of sizes, shapes and prices, light-weight and rugged, that can be assembled in a fraction of the time and effort than they once were. Grab your backpacks, your sleeping bags and portable stoves, pack plenty of food and drink to keep you going, and head off into the wilderness. It is not unheard of for adventuresome families to set up camp in idyllic spots in the mountains, near a beach or lake where they remain from days or weeks at a time, at minimal cost. Now, that's hard to beat!

Campsites

For those looking for something slightly less intrepid, there is always the option of staying at a privately or publicly run campsite that can be found almost anywhere in the Western world, kitted out with bathroom and kitchen facilities. Some of the fancier ones include playgrounds and swimming pools, marked hiking trails and even cafes and grocery stores. Obviously, the key advantage to this option over a hotel stay is the cost.

Despite Sam being raised in a national park in New Zealand, and much of my upbringing spent in the rugged Canadian wilderness, our kids have had more experience with well-equipped campsites in Western Europe than in the forests of our home countries. We were first introduced to this style of camping when Sam and I got married almost twenty years ago. We were on a tight budget but dreamed of enjoying an extended European honeymoon. Our solution came in the form of a cheap tent and double sleeping bag purchased at a French suburban superstore. Without doing any research at all, we found conveniently situated campsites in Germany, Switzerland, Austria and France that brought us close the places we wanted to explore.

ADVANTAGES OF NEPALESE CAMPING

My friend, Debbie, adds *"one of the advantages of trekking in Nepal is that you don't have to haul all your camping equipment with you, if you don't want to. Our family simply stayed in teahouses en route. They were nothing fancy, but we didn't have camping gear to contend with."*

I agree with Debbie that this is a real bonus, particularly if trekking in the Himalayas is only part of your travel plans. Camping equipment is heavy and cumbersome and can add a lot to your luggage load.

Glamping

Recently, it has become a family tradition of ours to camp along the Dordogne River in the south of France. Our campsite of choice sits in Sarlat-le-Caneda, a hobbit-like village carved out of the rock face. Up and down the river stand spectacular medieval castles and hamlets in perfect view from our rented kayaks. It's impossible to over-exaggerate the beauty of this place.

Aptly referred to as *glamping*, it's nothing like the rough and rugged camping Sam and I were raised with. Fine camping accoutrement is displayed by our campsite neighbors right down to quality silverware, table cloths, flower vases and crystal glassware, quality local wine, ironed and elegant *adventure wear* complemented by (we like to believe) sophisticated conversation. No matter how hard we try to blend in, we never fail to roll out of our tents in the morning looking disheveled and crumpled, as though we slept on the floor of a damp cave, just like any good Canadian-Kiwi family is apt to do.

If you're considering adding a bit of European glamping to your itinerary, here are some websites to begin your campsite search:

- campingfrance.com
- eurocampings.co.uk
- eurocamp.co.uk

KAYAKING THROUGH A HOBBIT-LIKE LAND.
DORDOGNE, FRANCE

Just add water

A nice spin on a standard camping vacation can include white-water rafting, like we have enjoyed in New Zealand, Bali and along the Colorado River in Utah. Some adventures last just a few hours, but many outfitters offer trips ranging from days to weeks, including meals and camping equipment. Unsurprisingly, there are a huge range of options in the Grand Canyon. Age restrictions are largely determined by the size of the rapids and the season you go. Some offer tours for kids as young as 6-years old.

ADVENTURE TRAVEL – A KEY INGREDIENT TO ANY FAMILY'S GAP YEAR.
TONGARIRO RIVER, NEW ZEALAND

Rooftop camping

And then there's truck rooftop camping, which we were introduced to in Namibia. It has become, without a doubt, my favourite way to travel!

There is nothing like waking to an African sunrise and the rumble of a lion's roar in the distance. Sleeping out in a tent allows one to feel part of what is most thrilling about Africa. The continent does come with its fair share of small animals, reptiles and insects that can easily crawl into a sleeping bag. For that reason, we made the superb decision of renting a Toyota 4X4 fitted with two tents that sat securely on the roof of the vehicle. The tents were easily unfolded in the evening and equally easily packed up in the morning. As seasoned campers, we found them entirely comfortable, and wonderfully exotic.

MY KINDA PARADISE.
SOSSUSVLEI, NAMIBIA

The truck came with all the supplies we required, right down to a small fridge, stove, table, chairs and cooking supplies, all for an unexpectedly reasonable price. We camped in a variety of campsites speckled around the country, each equipped with bathroom facilities and personal-use barbeques. Despite these conveniences, camping under the stars did bring us face-to-face with the African wilds.

One night we heard a splash in the swimming pool that had been carved out of the desert floor just yards from our camp. The light of our flashlights failed to spot any glowing eyes in the dark, which visitors to Africa are instructed to check for, but we heard the distinct sound of splashing. It turned out that an impressively-sized male gemsbok had fallen into the pool while drinking from it, and we could vaguely see him flailing about. This was our cue to act. While the kids and I hopped around at one side of the pool, clapping our hands, the gemsbok struggled to get to the shallow end where Sam grab onto its sharp antler and, with one strong heave, managed to pull the sodden animal out of the water. Sam then leapt back to avoid getting pierced as the gemsbok escaped into the darkness. It was only then that our eyes adjusted to the moonlight and we could see eight or so stupefied gemsbok surrounding us silently waiting their turns to drink from the campsite pool.

Back through the darkness, onto the truck rooftop, tent flaps zipped tight, our face-to-face encounter with African wildlife left us feeling quietly intrepid.

A GROUP OF GEMSBOK CONVENIENTLY POSING FOR OUR CAMERA.
NAMIBI

Numerous recommendations on truck rental companies can be found on sites like *TripAdvisor.* We chose to go with *Cardboard Box,* and were entirely satisfied with their service.

WARNING:

If you decide to add camping in Africa to your itinerary, keep your shoes inside the tent at night. I made the mistake of leaving my hiking sandals out only to find that a local jackal had run off with them in the night, leaving only her distinctive footprints behind.

Remember to shake your shoes out in the morning in case a little creature moved in while you slept.

GER CAMPING IN MONGOLIA

Vivian and her husband, John, took their children to Mongolia not once but three times. *"I always saw myself as a city person,"* Vivian explained, *"but it was so beautiful . . . we just had to keep returning."*

How old were your kids when you went to Mongolia?

"The first time our youngest was three, and oldest five. We returned the next year and two years later. It was an easy flight up to the Mongolian capital, Ulan Batur (UB), from Beijing, where we were living at the time."

Where did you stay?

"We spent a short time in UB, to visit the Soviet-style Natural History Museum, which we really enjoyed. But most of the time we stayed a few hours out of the city at a ger (round canvas Mongolian tent) camp. The camp staff arranged our transportation and provided meals in the ger canteen. We had simple beds, and wood burners in each ger for the nights, as they can get very cold. Everything was arranged for us."

When did you go?

"We went in the summer, in June and July, when the weather is at its best. (It can get very cold during the rest of the year.) We also timed it so we could attend the annual Naadam festival, when Mongolians compete in traditional wrestling, horseback riding and archery. It was special to see."

What was the food like?

"Mutton, mutton, mutton. Oh, and delicious yak milk yogurt . . . and smelly yak butter – not so delicious. A real meat and potatoes diet . . . hardy winter fare."

What was the best part of your Mongolia adventures?

"It was so beautiful. We road horseback without saddles, just blankets. No bridle, or stirrups, or helmet . . . In those wide-open spaces the kids could run and run in any direction and we never had to stop them. We could always see them. There was nothing to do, but within a day the kids found that they could entertain themselves for hours with a single rope or a stick that they had found. It was so liberating for all of us."

Do you have any advice for parents considering this trip?

"You need to be flexible about hygiene. Don't be too precious. Your kid might come back with a goat skull and you just have to go along with it."

Any final thoughts?

"The people were so incredibly warm. I get nostalgic just thinking about it."

Self-contained canal cruises

If slowly cruising through Europe appeals to you, where you can view spectacular castles and quaint villages as you go, consider including a canal cruise in your itinerary. Self-contained canal boats include their own kitchen, bathroom and sleeping quarters, as well as open-air decks where you can sit back and enjoy the view gently pass by.

Our kids and their paternal grandparents went on their own tour along the Canal du Midi in France. The highlight of the trip was managing their way through the many ancient locks en route.

Ireland and Great Britain are other popular destinations for river barge cruises. To begin your research, see:

- bargesinfrance.com
- gobarging.com
- canalholidays.com

THE KIDS AND THEIR KIWI GRANDPARENTS, ADY & PETE,
ABOUT TO NEGOTIATE A CANAL LOCK.
CANAL DU MIDI, FRANCE

GUIDED TOURS

In recent years, we've come around to the idea of guided tours, much to my surprise. The image of exhausted-looking tourists, attired in matching baseball caps, piling on and off buses to take their requisite selfies in front of the Great Wall before being swarmed by hawkers, had always filled me with dread. But that's not the guided tour I mean. Rather, what we have managed to enjoy in a variety of locations in Europe, Africa and Asia are knowledgeable locals who introduce us to places and experiences otherwise inaccessible to tourists.

It started a few years ago when Sam and I visited Xinjiang, the north-western most province of China. It is an immense place, with a fascinating history, where cultures meet at the heart of the ancient Silk Road. The local people here are Uyghurs, Muslims who speak a cousin of Turkish, and are blessed with exotic facial features - a blend of Asian and Caucasian. This is the original Melting Pot!

We found that the benefits of private guides in this region – one in Kashgar and the other in Urumqi and Turpan - included having us brought directly to remarkable historical sites and markets, and hours of conversation about local culture and history. Most enjoyable was being welcomed into people's homes where we were introduced to authentic Uyghur cuisine and customs. Such a rich experience could not have been possible had we been on our own or in a group tour.

Similarly, we explored Xiahe, Gansu province in the Tibetan plateau with the English-speaking wife of a former nomad. She and her driver made it possible for us to explore the immense grassland region away from the tour buses and set itineraries, and learn about the people who live in the region said to be *More Tibetan than Tibet*. The highlight of our tour was an impromptu tea break in the *ger* (tent) of a gracious nomadic woman we stumbled upon in the grasslands far from anywhere.

SMILES AND BASIC SIGN LANGUAGE ARE UNIVSERAL.
GANSU, CHINA

TOUR GUIDES & YOUNGER KIDS

Daniela explains that *"when visiting historic sites when our two boys were young, we found that investing in guides to take us around was a worthwhile expense, as the kids tended to listen more than if Mom or Dad were reading a description from the Lonely Planet guide book. The kids usually connected well with the tour guides, were able to ask questions, and became much more engaged in the whole experience. We did this in Angkor Wat, Bagan, Florence, Rome, Bangkok, Bali, and Yogjakarta."*

In the above cases, we found our guides through online searches, starting with, but not limited to, *TripAdvisor*. Simply type in the location – country, city, town or region - you plan to visit, and key words like *guide* or *tour*. Reviews from fellow travelers on this website have provided us with invaluable advice and unexpected travel ideas.

How we found our guide in Opuwo, Namibia was different. An employee at our lodge, who had helped us with a minor car problem, knew *a guy who knows a guy who might be able to help [you] visit the village of either the Himba or Herero tribes.* A quick couple of phone calls later and we were on our way to one of the best travel days of our lives.

Wedding Crashers in Namibia – by Sam

As promised, Uatiza (Michael)Hepute was waiting at the supermarket where we were instructed to buy cooking oil and massive sacks of sadza - white corn meal which forms the staple of every meal – which would soon be presented as gifts at the villages we were heading to. Three sisters of his Herero community were getting married that morning and he had arranged for us to attend the ceremony. It was an amazing honor that we immediately felt entirely underdressed for, but honored beyond belief.

Half an hour or so down the highway, through scrubland and thick sand, I was finally given a reason to engage the four-wheel drive I'd been longing to try out. Past acres of thorn trees we emerged into a clearing and the Herero village we'd been aiming for. The Herero people are traditionally farmers and ranchers, raising cattle for food, sale, dowries and as indications of status, and while now they're often teachers, ministers, hairdressers and truck drivers, the village of their birth and their clan remains the central point of their lives, bringing them back for occasions such as today's wedding. Despite fighting at least two wars with the occupying Germans in the early 1900s, the Herero enthusiastically adopted the style of dress common to their occupiers, and wear it to this day. Men in long-sleeved shirts, trousers and trilby hats. Women in enormous dresses down to their ankles and wide, flat hat/headdresses - so it was a large crowd of people dressed in this way that we saw gathering in the village.

The bride and groom were sitting under a large tent to shade everyone from the sun, the bride looking utterly miserable, the groom not much happier. Michael explained that tradition dictates that the bride joins her husband's family/village/clan, and is probably sad at the prospect of leaving her family. Speaking with her father - a recently retired headmaster - he told me "Oh, she's supposed to look miserable. Actually, she's fine - her husband's village is not that far away and its closer to where she works."

After songs and prayers lead by the bridesmaids from the (Lutheran, of course) church, the ceremony then turned back to the ancient traditions of the Herero, gathering around the Holy Fire, the central point of the village. The extended members of both families gathered tightly together and shuffled incredibly slowly towards the center of the village and sat next to a large pile of carefully cut and stacked branches of sacred wood - the Holy Fire. The chief of the bride's village (the headmaster we spoke with earlier) and the other senior men asked the men of the groom's village about his character and made it clear that the wedded couple's happiness was the responsibility of everyone. The women all sat in a close-knit pack, sweating in the heat of the direct sun, and mostly keeping silent except for occasionally voicing support for the bride. The chief nodded his assent and that was it, the crowd stood up and began to prepare to return to Opuwo or their own villages.

FORMAL DRESSES TODAY RECALL NAMIBIA'S GERMAN COLONIAL
PERIOD FROM THE 1890'S.
NAMIBIA

SHARING THE SHADE WITH SOME OF THE CHARMING
GENTLEMEN OF THE HERARO WEDDING PARTY.
NAMIBIA

Just when we thought our experience at the Herero wedding couldn't be topped, Michael directed us to a village of the Himba tribe. Painted head to toe in *otjize* paste, a mixture of butterfat and ochre pigment, used to protect themselves from the harsh sun, and to keep clean in a region where water is scarce. The women's heads were partially shaved, apart from long dreadlocks caked in otjize. These incredible people were, by far, the most exotic we had ever encountered.

Their tiny village consisted of eight or so round, clay huts topped with thatch. The community was surrounded by sharp, craggy, fantastically-woven wooden fences, designed as much to keep the wildlife out as the livestock in. Playful children, bare-chested and loin-clothed, greeted us as we entered, and immediately dragged our two kids, beaming, into their fun.

HIMBA GIRLS.
NAMIBIA

While Michael translated, Sam and I conversed with the ladies about their lives. Like other Namibians we had met in our journey thus far, they were amused by Sam's hairy arms. These traditional Himba ladies were also critical of how our guide, a Himba himself, adorned his dreadlocks in more of a Jamaican style. While they sat in front of their huts, beading ankle bracelets with leather and metal pellets, they took little notice of their tiny children climbing onto my lap to get a better look at themselves in my reflective sunglasses.

The otjize on the lady's hands and legs left a powdery copper finish on their handiwork. I didn't need much convincing to purchase some of these gorgeous pieces, saving the women the trouble of transporting them into town for sale, while instantaneously becoming some of my most treasured possessions.

By the time we left that tiny Himba village, we were dizzy with excitement. It was, without a doubt, our most memorable day as world travelers. And it could never have had happened without our superb guide, Uatiza (Michael) Hepute.

ANOTHER UNIVERSAL TRUTH - THERE'S NO GREATER FUN THAN BEING SWUNG AROUND BY A BIG BOY.
NAMIBIA

LAST CHANCE TO SEE

Here's one more thing to consider as you bounce around itinerary ideas - unspoilt travel destinations are becoming rare. If there is something you have long dreamed of seeing, go as soon as you can.

Sam and I can easily spout off a list of places we're relieved to have seen *before they changed.* One such place is Xiahe, China, the home of Labrang Monastery, one of the few and finest surviving Buddhist monasteries left on the Tibetan Plateau. Over the course of our few days there, we watched in horror as the foundations of an enormous tour bus parking lot were laid. It was clear that that remote spiritual gem would soon be going through the same tacky transformation as so many historical sites in China have in recent years. I now worry for Cambodia, Laos, Myanmar, Peru, Namibia and a weighty list of other precious destinations soon to succumb to the destructive pressures of global tourism.

Go now, while you still can, and bear witness, before the karaoke bars and neon arrive, and all that is authentic is commercialized.

Along the same lines, there are no guarantees how long many of the pearls of the natural world will be with us. My friend Katrina, a world-renowned wildlife conservationist, offers this abbreviated list of natural treasures worth seeing while you still can:

- Mountain gorillas in Rwanda
- Cheetahs in Namibia
- Wildlife migration in the Serengeti
- Galapagos Islands
- Amazon rainforest
- Machu Picchu, Peru

Elephants, rhinos and giraffes are but a few of the African species under threat, and may not be around for future generations. Significant areas of the Great Barrier Reef are now dead. As the ice continues to melt in northern Canada, the numbers of polar bears are rapidly diminishing. See them while you can, and then you and your family can advocate for them when you return home. With this idea in mind, please visit the Rhino Protection Trust website at rhinoprotectiontrust.com to see the good work they are doing to protect the highly vulnerable South African rhino. This is a group our family spent time with in the Limpopo region, and they need support to continue their good work.

FAMILY TRAVEL OPTIONS

There are many excellent resources available today to help find travel options for your unique family. I recommend taking your time browsing the travel section of your favorite bookstore. Then, move on to the ever-increasing number of excellent websites that specialize in family travel. Sign-up for their email newsletters and blogs that most appeal to your family's travel style.

Here are just a few websites you might try, or simply type in *family travel newsletters/blogs* and explore the long list that comes up.

- Walking on Travels
- Discover Corps
- Globe Trotting Mama
- So Many Places
- ZZZ World Ninjas
- Vagabond Family.org

5 TAKE-AWAYS

1. Weigh the pros and cons of taking your young child on a historical or cultural holiday. While she is less likely to remember the details of the trip, the mere experience of seeing new and different things can make it worthwhile. An older child or teen is probably better equipped to grasp and remember the significance of those experiences.

2. Beach vacations can be some of the least expensive options for traveling families with children of any age. Consider including activities like kite surfing, snorkeling, sea kayaking, sailing or scuba diving in the mix.

3. There are many different approaches to family camping vacations, including wilderness tent camping, campsite camping and upscale *glamping*, camper vanning/RVing, *ger* and truck rooftop camping. Consider what other activities you might include in such a trip, like whitewater rafting, canoeing, cycling, hiking, caving or kayaking.

4. A personal tour guide, with local knowledge and connections, can make your visit to a foreign place even more memorable.

5. Consider including places likely to change soon in your itinerary. Try to predict where tourism industries have yet to take hold, but soon will. Think about natural locations that are under threat, where time is running out to enjoy them.

Chapter 4

Family Volunteering

"AFRICA IS NOW OFFICIALLY MY FAVORITE CONTINENT." SCOUT, AGE 12
SOUTH AFRICA

If you are interested in including something a bit different in your family's travel itinerary, consider volunteering. It can be an opportunity to get close and personal with the places and people you are visiting, and to learn first-hand about things entirely new and different. Moreover, it gives you a chance of coming away from the experience feeling like you've contributed something worthwhile.

All too often on previous trips I felt detached from the places we were passing through, particularly when we were barreling down a highway at 100km/h. Viewing scenery through a windscreen is not much different from watching a show on the Discovery Channel, it seems to me, except that with TV you get a narrated explanation of what you're viewing. For this tour, we were finally able to invest some focused attention on the locations we had flown across the world to visit. Nowhere was that more apparent than in our two-month tour of Southern Africa, which included volunteering in three different places.

These days, tourists can find hundreds, perhaps thousands, of volunteer opportunities – hence the term *voluntourism* - located all over the world, in an assortment of fields, from wildlife conservation to house building, from education to caring for the homeless. Some of these accept youngsters accompanied by responsible adults.

Although not always the case, volunteer-abroad experiences generally have a fee attached. Participants may be expected to cover the cost of accommodation and meals, plus pay a bit extra to go toward the running of the organization. Prices vary according to location, facilities and length of stay.

Keep in mind when doing your research that less credible organizations are more interested in making a profit than doing good. I have no magic formula for working out which to go with. In our case, I simply paid attention to the testimonials made available to me and used my intuition to gauge the authenticity in the correspondence I received. And I'm pleased to report that we were delighted with all three experiences chosen.

After weeks of scrolling through websites and sending out inquiry emails, I settled on two agents – *Enkosini Eco Experience* and *Africa Impact* – who liaised between us and the volunteer organizations we ended up choosing. They were a great help in working through the logistics, such as scheduling, permits and transportation. That said, if you find an organization with which you might like to volunteer, consider contacting them directly rather than going through an agent. This could potentially save you a bit of money.

Other people I know arranged their own volunteer experiences through personal connections, charities they already sponsored, as well as organizations or religious communities they were members of.

If you're interested in finding a volunteer experience at a reduced cost, seek advice and introductions from acquaintances who have already volunteered abroad. Send emails to organizations you feel are doing good in the world and offer your services. Who knows what interesting opportunities might present themselves?

Bambelela Monkey Rehabilitation Farm, South Africa

Going to Africa to experience the wildlife had been a dream of ours for years, but we were put off by how expensive safaris can run. It's not unheard of to be charged upwards of $1000 per person per night, which was way beyond our budget. Moreover, the idea of paying a small fortune to stay for only a few days in an opulent lodge, side by side with a bunch of Europeans and North Americans *(Nice people, but they're not who we came to meet in Africa....)*, and seeing animals only from a crowded tour vehicle held little appeal for us. That is why we signed on to be volunteers at *Bambelela Monkey Rehabilitation Farm* and *Siyafunda*, in Limpopo, South Africa.

YOU CAN'T TRY THIS AT HOME.
BAMABELELA MONKEY SANCTUARY, SOUTH AFRICA

Bambelela was our first stop in Africa, and could not have been further from a high-end safari tour. From the moment we arrived to find a troop of wild baboons drinking from the algae-green swimming pool, and wild warthogs standing guard along the entrance path, we knew we were in store for an authentic African experience.

Bambelela did not promise luxury, nor did we get it, although our family was housed in a comfortable African-fashioned chalet normally reserved for weekend visitors. We were four of 12 volunteers working at the sanctuary at the time. The others ranged in age from their early twenties to late forties. Some stayed for a few days and others for a number of years, off and on, never getting quite enough of the 350 plus vervet monkeys and baboons cared for at the facility.

Silke von Eynern established Bambela in 2003 with the sole purpose of caring for injured and orphaned vervets and baboons, and rehabilitating as many as possible back into the South African wild. The facility is run on a shoestring and we have no doubt that every cent paid for this unique experience went toward helping the animals.

From 7:45a.m. each morning until well into evening, we prepared utterly disgusting primate meals, cleaned poop off floors and climbing equipment, built and painted cages, dug holes, and then, to make it all worthwhile, cuddled and cared for orphaned and handicapped monkeys.

It did not take long before we got used to wild baboon troops passing by just yards away, or families of ornery warthogs rummaging through the grass along the path between the facility and our chalet. Giant porcupines would hunker down near us during evening staff meetings under the African stars, and zebra, kudu and impala would regularly be seen making their way through the bush barely a hundred yards away.

It's not for everyone!

Despite being a genuine animal lover, I admit that the proximity to the baboons and monkeys unnerved me. I did not expect that. There were plenty of little bites and scratches, and unpredictable bouncy animal activity, such as jumping on my head and climbing down my shirt. The kids loved every minute of that. They would sit for hours with monkeys cuddled on their laps, tucked in their shirts or wrapped around their necks having their scalps groomed by tiny primate fingers.

Declan and Scout literally matured before our eyes during those extraordinary weeks at Bambelela. Whereas I was overly-cautious in dealing with the screaming, leaping, nibbling, adorable monkeys, the kids were right in the middle of it. Their enthusiasm made them the perfect participants, taking every bit of it in their strides.

Furthermore, warm relationships developed between the kids and the other long-term and serial volunteers and staff. They were unique characters, the lot of them, impressively knowledgeable about the primates they were working with, and open to sharing everything they knew. Our kids spent long hours with these people every day, engaged in conversations and working alongside them as peers. The experience built a confidence and maturity in our children that was quite remarkable to witness over such a short time.

Likewise, the work ethic they showed was impressive, and quite simply, surprising. Regardless of how difficult or disgusting the chores they were assigned, they were right in there. The kids were expected to work just like the other volunteers did, and few accommodations were made due to their ages. This was entirely fine with them. Every evening the kids rolled up to our chalet dirty, and exhausted, smelling like monkeys, laughing and sharing their stories.

ELBOW-DEEP IN UTTERLY DISGUSTING PRIMATE FOOD.
BAMABELA, SOUTH AFRICA

In retrospect, would we have done it again? Would we have included weeks of monkey chaos and filth in our world tour itinerary? *Absolutely!* is the kids' enthusiastic response. In addition to it now being Scout's favorite place on this planet, it tore us out of our comfort zones like nothing we had experienced before, and taught us an immense amount about animals, and monkeys in particular, wildlife conservation and, almost more profoundly, ourselves.

I have also come to learn that there are many ways to volunteer. Next time, I may offer to assist Silke in other ways, perhaps using my background in business to help attract funding to the sanctuary. *I've had quite enough of monkey poo and repulsive baboon feed, thank you very much.* While Sam says *I'll happily return to fixing cages and shoveling monkey s**t.* The kids will re-establish themselves as honorary members of a monkey troop, where they will follow the codes of primate hierarchy, beginning close to the bottom of the rung once again, and feeling entirely at home.

WARNING:

If any of your family members are fussy about cleanliness, food quality, close quarters, hard work or animals, this is probably not the experience for you. Then again, if your family is looking for something genuinely different, challenging, intense and educational, and wonderfully rewarding, then you might want to consider it. The rough edges are a refreshing contrast to the comfortable, screen-addicted existences so many city kids live today. It will toughen up just about anybody, in most gratifying and memorable ways.

bambelela.org.za

Siyafunda @ Makalali Wildlife Reserve, South Africa

AN EVENING OF ANIMAL VIEWING WITH OUR FORMIDABLE GUIDE, EMMA. MAKALALI, SOUTH AFRICA.

Like Bambalela, *Siyfunda* at *Makalali Wildlife Reserve* was recommended to us by *Enkosini Eco Experience* as being ideal for families, although an entirely different wildlife experience.

Each morning at 5a.m. we, the other volunteers and one of our expert trackers, Emma Jenkins (pictured above) or Michael Job, the reserve owner (think Crocodile Dundee with a South African accent), would jump aboard an open-air Land Rover on a rough and dusty four-hour African safari, only to have it repeated during the sunset hours. Our role was to sight animals and record their GPS location coordinates, the numbers of each species spotted, their gender and general behaviors. This data was then collated and shared with research institutions in the US and UK, including the World Wildlife

Fund (WWF). Although the original focus of Siyfunda was to conduct research in elephant contraception, as volunteers we gathered data on all of the Big Five (lions, buffalo, leopards, rhinos and elephants) and other species found on the reserve.

On our very first morning, following a lesson on tracking animals using their footprints, we came across an adolescent bull elephant casually making his way up the track toward our Land Rover, followed by another, and then, within a few short minutes, over 30 members of two herds of the most magnificent beasts we had ever laid our eyes on. It was, quite simply, awe-inspiring. And this was just the beginning!

SOME OF OUR WILDLIFE COUNTS WERE EASIER, AND MORE AWE-INSPIRING, THAN OTHERS.
SOUTH AFRICA.

Giraffes, zebra, impala, kudu, wildebeest and buffalo were just a sample of the animals we would come across on an almost daily basis. Spotting lions was particularly thrilling, lying in the shade with their stomachs full, or immediately after a kill, their faces covered in blood, taking turns eating through a fallen waterbuck.

It was astounding how much we learnt about African animals over those few short weeks – their behaviors, mating habits, survival strengths and challenges, their predators and prey. We were also schooled in how to survive in, and share, the habitat with the Big Five, as well as about the tragic reality of poaching in South Africa. It was the ultimate wildlife learning experience for older kids and adults alike.

Our modest accommodation at the Makalali camp was nothing to write home about, but our priority was to have an adventure, and we were comfortable enough. If luxury had been our priority, we would have chosen one of the many pricey lodges that speckle the Limpopo region, but I question if we would have had a better wildlife experience at any of those places. Besides, we think it's important that kids be adaptable and not expect 5-star living. (Next time, Sam and I plan to sleep outside on the high, open platform, under the stars, to silently view the nocturnal wildlife pass by.)

WILDLIFE DATA COLLECTION SUPPORTS ACADEMIC RESEARCH.
SOUTH AFRICA

It's not for everyone!

Our time spent at Makalali Wildlife Reserve was amazing but, to be sure, it is not for everyone. If any of your family members are unnerved by large animals, insects or snakes, you should think twice about this kind of adventure.

When the sun goes down in Africa, it's time to turn your flashlights on and check your path carefully for the glowing eyes of nocturnal predators. We found this thrilling, but it can certainly rub against the fear thresholds of many cautious travelers.

On our last night, two bull elephants came a stone's throw from our chalet to devour the delicious shrubbery around the compound. After careful observation by our highly-competent field guide, it was confirmed that the animals posed no threat at that time. But elephants, like all wild animals in Africa, are unpredictable. Humans need to show them respect and follow the proper rules of *bushveld* conduct, at all times. I highly discourage any family with small children, or children who have trouble following instructions closely, or keeping quiet when the time calls for it, from participating in this type volunteer program. For anyone else, it's an experience of a lifetime.

JUST MINUTES AFTER A WATERBUCK FEAST. MAKALALI WILDLIFE RESERVE
SIYAFUNDACONSERVATION.COM

Lion Encounter - *Africa Impact, Zimbabwe*

Our time in Victoria Falls, Zimbabwe fulfilled a lifelong dream of mine - to help children and women in Africa. It was, quite frankly, the most intensely heartwarming period of my travel life, just as I imagined it would be. The time sped by and every member of our family wished we could have stayed longer. When a Zimbabwean medicine man predicted that I would return to his country 11 more times, Sam and I vowed on the spot that we would make that happen.

I found *Africa Impact,* an agent for a variety of voluntourism projects in Africa, through a laborious internet search. I was specifically seeking a community service program that would allow our children to get directly involved. It just so happened that their partners in Victoria Falls, *Lion Encounter* and *ALERT*, had recently opened their community program to families.

WALKING LION CUBS BEFORE THEIR EVENTUAL RELEASE INTO THE SEMI-WILD.
LION ENCOUNTER, ZIMBABWE

Lion Encounter was established to help grow the lion population in the region. Fee-paying volunteers over the age of 18 assist in the rehabilitation of lions back into the semi-wild. Most of our fellow volunteers were there to do just that, but it was not an option for us given our kids' ages. We had just completed several glorious weeks experiencing African wildlife in South Africa and Namibia, so were content directing our attention exclusively toward working with and for local people.

To tell the truth, I did baulk at the thought of taking the children to Zimbabwe, a country with a recent history of violence and severe economic turmoil. It was only through a long string of emails and assurances from Africa Impact and Lion Encounter that Victoria Falls is a safe place that we agreed to go. It turned out to be a lovely town where we felt more comfortable, welcome and safe than in many other places in the world, including the US.

Each morning, we and three or four other community volunteers would head to one of the various sites, including a town preschool and a tiny rural one, a primary school, an orphanage, a home for the elderly and a garden run by and for carriers of HIV/AIDS.

CARRYING WATER THIS WAY IS HARDER THAN IT LOOKS!
ZIMBABWE
(SCOUT LEADS, FOLLOWED BY OUR GARDENING TEACHER, MS. GRACE, AND
FELLOW VOLUNTEER KRISTIE, WHILE I BRING UP THE REAR.)

To say that we felt welcome cannot be overly exaggerated. Everyone we met, from the beaming children and their dedicated teachers, to the elderly folks and the ladies who have committed their lives to care for them, to the people living with HIV/AIDS, to the Lion Encounter team who worked tirelessly to help the needy in their community, let us know that they appreciated our being there. Every volunteer was excited to help, and we all quietly felt that we were getting more out of the priceless experience than we were actually putting in.

At the schools and orphanage, we would read, talk and sing with the children, play games and run lessons. I think the children particularly benefitted from learning to speak and write English directly from native-English speakers.

We did basic gardening work for the people living with HIV/AIDS, which included carrying water from the communal well. We all tried transporting 20lbs water buckets on our heads with varying degrees of success - a skill that looks far easier when the local ladies do it.

For the elderly, in addition to helping clean around their compound and cut firewood, perhaps our most important role was simply to spend time with them, to listen to their stories and show them that they were not forgotten and we cared about them.

All of the ladies running the schools, the orphanage and the elderly people's home were doing so out of the goodness of their hearts, as they were either paid a pittance or nothing at all for their efforts. For that reason alone, it felt right to lend them a well-deserved hand.

While the kids and I focused on teaching, Sam got busy doing physical work around the facilities, like cutting concrete-hard African firewood and fixing broken playground equipment.

Declan and Scout were utterly in their elements. The little children hung off our big, strong son like he was a walking, laughing playground jungle gym. When he wasn't wrestling with a half-dozen of them on the ground, they would be piled high on his lap while he read Dr. Seuss and classic nursery rhymes. Scout's forte turned out to be leading sing-alongs and running lessons on English phonetics.

Our two kids were treated with such warmth and enthusiasm that they did not show a hint of apprehension about taking on the role of teacher, regardless of their students' ages. In fact, they were probably more popular with the local children than we adults were simply because it was such a novelty for them to spend time with such young, playful *teachers.*

PLAYTIME & READING TIME WITH DECLAN.
ZIMBABWE

We were comfortably housed in a well-equipped and guarded compound near the town center. During our stay, there were anywhere from 15 to 20 fun-loving volunteers staying at the compound, most of whom were there to work at the lion facility.

All-in-all, our experience of community volunteering in Zimbabwe was a heartwarming success. We have all agreed that it is worth a revisit, soon.

lionencounter.com/volunteer

CHANGING LIVES

Of all the precious times we enjoyed around the world, I think the whole family would agree that our weeks in Africa were the most life-changing. To this day we get choked up reflecting on our time there. As we flew out of Johannesburg airport, the kids vowed to return to volunteer during their pre-university gap years, but I hope our family can fit in another visit during at least one more summer or Christmas vacation before then.

Declan's dreams are now filled with heaping portions of mouth-watering warthog, *I kid you not*. Scout's future aspirations swing between doing hands-on animal conservation work and running schools in Africa. I wouldn't be surprised if she ended up doing both. A full and rich life rarely travels in a straight line.

5 TAKE-AWAYS

1. Volunteering abroad can be an excellent way for you and your family to have a unique, personal experience with the people and place you're visiting.

2. Research well in advance volunteer organizations that take children, as most do not.

3. Ask for a realistic description of what will be required of each family member before registering. Determine whether the program matches your goals, strengths and interests. Ask how much downtime is given per day, what the facility and accommodations are like, and how food is managed – whether food is provided or if volunteers are expected to purchase their own food at local markets.

4. Be realistic about how much your child is prepared to participate in the volunteer program. Match the volunteer program to your child's interests. Most programs that allow children deal with educating or playing with other children, assisting the elderly or working with animals.

5. Bring your positive attitude with you. Be realistic and flexible about the accommodation and food that comes with your volunteer experience.

Chapter 5

Age Matters

It's a sad truth that kids don't always want to do the same things as their parents do. They might not actually get the same kick out of touring a mausoleum of a former Communist dictator, or visiting a world-famous Tabasco factory, as you might. They might occasionally want a pool at their hotel, or to participate in an elephant ride tour with a group of elderly German tourists rather than drink cappuccino at a fabulous 19th century coffee bar that reminds you of a Summerset Maugham novel. *(Do I sound bitter? I don't mean to.)*

That said, I am the first to admit that we were lucky that our kids are only 18-months apart in age, and have an equally easy-going attitude toward new things. During our gap year, we did not have to deal with the challenges of balancing strikingly different needs or interests in our children, which many families undoubtedly do. I can only suggest that parents keep their kids' ages, habits and temperaments in the forefront of their minds while planning their tour, because the last thing anyone wants is to share close quarters 24-hours a day, for several weeks or months, with a miserable kid. As my friend Daniela explains of her own family's travel philosophy, *It's everyone's vacation, so it's important that everyone has fun!*

Pre-emptive measures

Having travelled to so many places with our children since they were infants, we recognize that each stage provides its own rewards, and challenges. Preparing for a successful journey often requires anticipating where your kid's greatest joys and struggles will enter the picture.

Ask yourself questions about your child like:

- *What is likely to be the highlight of that location for her?*
- *How much physical activity will he need each day? How will he get it?*
- *When is she likely to get bored, grumpy or tired? How can we be ready for that?*
- *Is she the right age for that activity?*
- *Is there any way to adapt the experience so he can enjoy it, too?*
- *Does he have any worries or phobias we need to prepare for?*
- *How will we deal with her unique eating or sleeping habits?*
- *Since she wants to do that, what can we do for him so both kids will be happy?*
- *What messages can we communicate to her before we head off to make her cooperative and a joy to travel with?*
- *How can we convince the kids that it is our [parents'] holiday, too, and that they need to be flexible when it's our turn to have fun?*

Disclaimer

I am not a child psychologist and won't pretend to know how your child will respond to the particular travel itinerary you're planning. The coming pages simply provide anecdotal responses to common issues about traveling with children raised by parents interviewed for this book.

I hope that this chapter gets you thinking about how you might prepare yourself and your youngster for what lay ahead, and preempt struggles that discourage some families from traveling in the first place.

PREGNANCY & TODDLERS

Pregnancy did not discourage us from travelling those many years ago. In fact, after months of 24-hour a day morning sickness, the sixth and seventh months of my pregnancies brought on my *happy hormones,* which were ideal for travelling. I was up for just about anything! Declan was pretty much a big baby upon conception, yet I managed to remain comfortable enough for Sam and me to have wonderful time touring Japan together during my seventh-month of pregnancy. Then, when Declan was just 15-months old, and I was six months pregnant with Scout, we joined my parents for a brief sojourn to Rome and Tuscany. Once again, I felt unstoppable. The only real challenge I faced was eating according to my doctor's advice. She warned against eating soft cheeses and meats that had been left at room temperature (a common practice in southern Europe), as well as wheat and sugar. *I'm in Italy and I'm supposed to avoid pasta, pizza and gelato? Ouch!*

Whereas pregnancy was not the problem, having a little tyke with a lot of energy needing to be spent was. Taking baby Declan through the Vatican Museum and St. Peter's Basilica was not only painfully boring for him, it was highly stressful for us. We could not keep him quiet in the Sistine Chapel, despite the incessant *shhhusshs* from the wonderfully fashionable but severe-looking security staff. We rushed through our meals at restaurants as one tag-team member would take the baby for a walk while the other took a few bites. Then, *Switch!* Romantic it was not, until we made a few key changes.

As one might expect, Italy is speckled with gloriously-stocked delis and supermarkets. As soon as we were reminded of this, we gave up on restaurants and turned to picnicking. Meals were enjoyed under the trees in city parks and on country fields overlooking Tuscan villages. We spent our days outside, exploring ancient streets with Declan on Sam's back, and then resting in parks and playgrounds where our little one could run around. It turned out to be an ideal compromise which saved us money in the process. Admittedly, we did not see (or eat) all that Italy had to offer on that trip, but we did return to explore Rome in its full glory with both kids 10 years later.

> **TIPS**
>
> - *Bring a light, foldable picnic blanket in your day bag for ad hoc picnics and rest stops.*
> - *To save money on car rentals, bring your own child car seat as daily fees for car seat rentals can run quite high.*

Consider bringing your child's car seat onto the plane with you, if your child sleeps well in it. This can be more comfortable for a child than an airplane seat. Check with your airline in advance to confirm that this is allowed.

Over the years, I have met travelling couples with toddlers sailing around the world, wandering through remote country markets in North Vietnam, viewing the panoramic view from the Eiffel Tower and skiing down mountains in Canada. Still, there are plenty of people out there who are putting off their travel plans because of fears about travelling with infants. That's a shame. I know it can be done. I've seen it. We've done it.

PRIMARY-AGED KIDS

Declan and Scout were on international flights an average of three or four times a year since they were babies. By the time they had reached 10 and 11-years of age, they had each been to over 20 countries on four continents. Such is the life of an expat family living in Singapore and China!

We were by no means unusual in our community of friends who took full advantage of frequent national holidays, employers' generous vacation time and enticing locations within easy reach. For that reason, travelling with primary school-aged kids doesn't spook us at all. In fact, it feels entirely natural for a family to take their children to the ends of the Earth the minute school is let out.

Kids are often far more resilient than they're given credit for, and even more so than many adults already addicted to comfortable, predictable conditions. Our friends trekked in Nepal with their six-year olds with the help of hired Sherpas who carried their packs, camping equipment and even children, at times. Other acquaintances with primary school kids toured Sri Lanka on the rough for weeks – getting around by local buses and rickshaws, and staying at 2-star accommodations throughout.

Before striking ambitious plans off your travel itinerary for the sake of the kids, think carefully about whether your concerns are valid.

Experience teaches resilience

Oh, the public bathrooms our kids have used without a second thought that many faint-hearted adults would not dare enter. And with that comes an astonishing sense of parental pride.

We hired a guide to take us on an evening food tasting tour of Can Tho, Vietnam, where we explored the rubbery delights of cobra and crocodile in spicy sauce, amongst other exotic dishes. I am not a particularly adventurous eater myself, but did plan on trying at least one bite of everything, unless it was dog. I was concerned that our rapidly growing, and perpetually ravenous, 13-year old son would be too grossed out by the food options to eat and was going to return to the bungalow massively hungry. But to our delight, he ate without a fuss. Both kids tried the spicy reptilian dishes, mixed with generous portions of rice and vegetables, and by the end of the evening were satiated. Sam and I were impressed by how easily they had risen to the challenge.

This led us to thinking about how the kids had been behaving on the trip up to that point - relaxed and accepting of just about everything. Not even the sight of a South-East Asian cockroach the size of a giant snow pea warranted a sideways glance. We had come to realize that years of travel, particularly in the developing world, had made the kids comfortable in situations that would leave many adults feeling way out of their depths.

I don't think our two kids are unusual in this way. Through conversations with family and friends who have traveled extensively with their children, it sounds as though most kids simply adapt. The drip, drip, drip of variety over time seems to make kids more resilient and as such, easier to travel with. For families who are new to this way of living, but are keen to give it a try, consider following a graduated itinerary, beginning with easier, more familiar destinations before moving on to more exotic and trying ones over time.

Following that meal of crocodile and cobra in Can Tho, Scout and I used the restaurant washroom. Without mentioning it at the time, we both noticed that one of the cooks had propped herself on a short stool next to the bathroom entrance to slice vegetables in, admittedly, a pretty filthy passage way. The bathroom itself was worse. It had the hole-in-the-floor variety of toilet - which our family likes to refer to as a *squatter* - with a bucket of water and scoop as substitute for a flusher. Customers were expected to supply their own toilet paper, which is standard in that part of the world, and toss the *wipings* into an overflowing waste bin. The floors, walls and sink were decaying in the Vietnamese heat and humidity. It was, in all truth, the kind of bathroom that inhabit the nightmares of many queasy travelers. Scout is no such person. She entered, did her business and came out, without a mention of what she had witnessed. I had to chuckle at her laidback response, thinking of how many queasy 12-years olds I had known who would have squealed at the sight of those facilities and refused to use them.

As for her impressions about our meal of cobra and crocodile, she explained, *Well, it's not what I planned for [for dinner] but . . . well, I hadn't actually planned on anything.*

And perhaps that was the key. She hadn't planned what she might have for dinner just as she and Declan had few, if any, expectations about what we were going to do any given day. Both Scout and her brother were taking the whole experience in their strides. They had managed to achieve what I hoped they would - a go-with-the-flow attitude that made travel with them such a pleasure.

That's not to say that we didn't make some adjustments to keep the kids bearable to live with, if that simply meant occasionally keeping secrets.

One such time was when the palm branches surrounding our hut along the Mekong Delta brushed against the grass rooftop. At night, when we heard rustling overhead, I assured Scout that there was nothing to worry about as the branches where simply swaying in the breeze. That seemed to placate her, as I snuggly tucked the mosquito nets around our mattresses. What I hadn't told her until days later was that a small jungle rat had built a nest behind the mirror in our primitive bathroom. The mosquito nets were as much to keep him out as the insects. Once we moved on to our next destination, and I admitted why I was so keen to tuck those nets, she let out a brief screech in horror, but it was too late to make any more of a fuss than that.

That little lesson served her well, months later in Africa. Small rats fed on the food and animal waste around the monkey sanctuary we volunteered at, and it wasn't uncommon to spot furry little critters scurry past from one hiding place to the next. In no time, Scout was entirely at ease with wildlife of all varieties, and took little notice of the rodents beyond casually tossing a rat-hunting dachshund towards the monkey food to scare them off. In the end, it was I who was more likely to give off an alarmed scream when I caught sight of a small shadow darting past my feet.

THE FUSSY CHILD

All of that is well and good, but there's no way my kid would react that way. He likes things to be familiar, clean and comfortable, which is going to make travelling with him difficult!

I hear what you're saying. There is every chance that your child will not appreciate all the differences he encounters on your world tour. He may push aside his dinner because he saw chunks of raw meat displayed in a local market hours earlier. He might protest that his pillow feels like a hard beanbag, not like the fluffy down one he's used to. She may refuse to sleep in a tent because it's *cooooold*, until she finally crawls under the blankets. For parents who need to prepare for this kind of resistance, here are suggestions I've gathered from my community of seasoned travellers.

SCOUT'S CASUAL GLANCE AT A PASSING WILD BABOON.
BAMBALELA, SOUTH AFRICA

Be the example

DON'T YOU BE FUSSY!

I'm a firm believer that kids pick up on their parents' attitudes. If you have a can-do attitude, chances are your kids will learn to have the same. And if you're hungry enough, you'll eat anything. - Vivian

As the parent, try not to be too precious yourself. Your child takes her cues from you about how to react to the good, the bad, and the ugly of the places you visit.

On one family excursion out of Beijing, we traveled to Datong and Pingyao, China with my cousin, Sandy. This was her first time to that country and we were keen to give her a real adventure. The locations we took her to had few English-speaking tourists, but the local restaurants were preparing for their eventual arrival by adding translations to their menus. In many cases, the English versions sounded utterly disgusting. Determined not to be put off, we decided to approach the situation with humor and sought out the most horrendous sounding dishes we could find. Here is a genuine list of what we found:

- *Cold face wire*
- *Pimple boil*
- *Speculation is shifting*
- *Homemade garlic intestinal*
- *Hometown bowl bald*
- *Bamboo hong small yellow croaker*
- *Grilled prawn farmers*
- *Manuel cat ears*
- *Cask stupid chicken*

- *My red face school saliva chicken*
- *Clear cooks the bull's penis*

Did the dishes turn out to be delicious? Umm, not always. But the kids took their cues from us and found humor where there might otherwise be dread. And they ate.

This may be an extreme example, but the theory applies to whatever new or different things your family encounters on your travels. Perhaps you'll be surprised by the small size of the pricey hotel room you booked in an ancient city. Rather than complaining, explain to your kids that it's a small price to pay for being so close to famous ruins. *If they were to build a modern hotel here they'd have to knock down some of these old buildings. That would be a shame, wouldn't it? It's expensive because a lot of other people want to enjoy these historical treasures, too. We're lucky to be here!*

So, I recommend to parents again, look confident and fearless, and avoid getting offended, annoyed or grossed out. Teach your child to take a sense of adventure and resilience with him through life by being a credible example.

DEALING WITH A PICKY EATER

Vivian suggests that *parents dealing with a picky eater find out ahead of time what the staples of the country are - rice, potatoes, pasta, bread – and what peelable fruits are available. The bottom line is that kids might not eat the mutton off the bone, but they might eat boiled potatoes. They might not eat stir fried vegies, but they'll eat the orange segments.*

And there's no point in worrying about balanced organic meals during the trip. The kids will be fine! What they are learning will be part of who they become and how they develop as global citizens. A few unhealthy meals are a small price to pay for that!

Be prepared

The differences you and your child encounter while travelling can be unsettling, so think ahead about how you might pre-empt your kid's negative reactions. Traveling parents regularly bring along sanitary cloths to wipe down filthy surfaces and dirty hands. Our family carries a sarong or picnic blanket to use when no suitable seating is available. Other friends suggest taking extra clothing items to fend off the cold, *because a cold child is a miserable child.* And our family always has games - card games, Yahtzee, pads of paper and pens - to prevent boredom in restaurants and train stations.

Carrying healthy snacks in your day-bag is a good idea, in case you can't find anything for your child to eat. We have found that packaged nuts can be found in even the most remote locations. And keep bottled water on hand to drink and clean with.

. . . but not too prepared

I must counter my above point about preparedness with a simple warning - the more you accommodate your child's fussiness, the more likely you'll be stuck with it. *A 12-year old who is unwilling to sit on a dirty bench has learnt that reaction over time.* I would recommend, as much as possible, to gradually wean your kid off his set ways and expectations. This may take time, perhaps, but eventually the experience of travel should teach him that differences and newness can be fun, delicious, or simply ignored.

CLEANLINESS IS IN THE EYE OF THE BEHOLDER

Vivian noticed the difference in her perception of cleanliness one summer when she and her family enjoyed *ger* camping in Mongolia, followed by fishing and camping in Canada.

There was very little difference in the way the kids enjoyed their outdoor experiences in those two countries, just our [the adults'] perceptions of what was clean and acceptable. We seemed more concerned about the kids staying clean in Mongolia than in Canada, but we shouldn't have.

The lesson Vivian took from this is to keep her worries in perspective. *Just because you're in a foreign land, don't assume the dangers are significantly greater than what you're used to.*

Challenge & praise

I'm going to eat the Mopani worm so I can get a certificate from the chef. Take a photo of me eating it so I can shock my friends.

(Actual quote from Scout, Zimbabwe.)

Kids like to feel that they're daring. They want their friends to think they're brave and do adventurous things. Let your daughter know that you'll email Grandpa with the news of her being the first in the group to reach the top of that strenuous trail. Encourage your son to write a funny story about riding his bike into the sewer in Southern China *(True story!)*, so you can include it in your family album and laugh about it for years to come.

Recognize her courage. Praise his strength. Encourage her humour. Nurture his sense of adventure.

CRAVING COMFORT FOOD

Daniela admits that occasionally her kids *get tired of the local food and need some "comfort food", like pizza, or pasta... so we let them choose a "non-local" restaurant. But we quickly realize that chefs are often far better at making local dishes, with local ingredients, than trying to replicate the "Western dishes" with their own "twist".*

We've been served spaghetti with ketchup (instead of marinara sauce) and pizza with a base of chili sauce (sambal), instead of tomato sauce, topped with chilis.

So, the lesson is - stick with the local food!

Shared decision-making

My friend, Claire, describes how her teenage son *needs to know the details about where we're going, and what we're going to do, in order to feel comfortable. He wants to know what to expect before he commits to our plans.* Responding positively to her son's need for information has worked well for Claire's family, and has quelled resistance to their travel plans.

This reminded me of how Declan, during his elementary school years, needed to get a strong sense of what lay ahead before he could relax and enjoy himself. By the time we set off on our gap year, however, that was no longer the case. At 13 and then 14, he was genuinely happy to just go along with our plans and see where it took us. In fact, *The less I know the better!* he would mumble. That's why we were surprised that at the mature age of 15, he got it into his head to work out the route we would drive when we moved from Houston to Boston. We were planning a 10-day journey, visiting some of the prettier sites through the Deep South and up into New England. By his own volition, he spent hours researching picturesque drives through national parks and identified lovely towns recommended on travel sites. He declared that he would be our tour guide, and as Sam and I had no firm ideas about what we should see, Declan was free to manage much of the trip. It was great! He felt responsible and wholly enthusiastic about what could have otherwise been, from his perspective, *a long and tedious family car trip.*

How about your child?

- *Would she benefit from participating in planning the trip?*
- *Will including him in the planning process make him feel more excited, comfortable or less anxious about the trip?*
- *Would he enjoy choosing activities? Restaurants? Travel routes? Hotels?*
- *Shall we come up with a list of options and let her choose her favourite?*

PARTICIPATION VS. POWER STRUGGLES

Daniela tells me *We usually encourage the kids to research the locations we are going to visit ahead of time, and take turns picking places to eat. When everyone participates, there tend to be fewer power struggles!*

A PASSAGE TO INDIA

My cousin Seth and his wife, Allison, both teachers, thought carefully about how they would prepare their daughters, Avra age 9 and Camile age 6, for their trip of India.

We did a lot of front-loading to build excitement and thereby nip fussiness in the bud. First, we got a dry erase map and had the girls plot routes, look at countries and paths. They got very excited about that part, and learnt a lot also. That helped on the plane as we were not only able to monitor our route, but also remember the map at home and connect to the discussions we had beforehand.

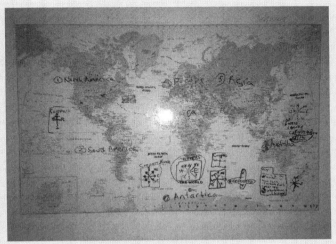

AVRA AND CAMILE'S PRE-TRIP MAP TO INDIA.

We also researched the destinations and gave the girls buy-in on what we would be doing and sites to see. This, again, eliminated them feeling as if they were tagging along on our adventures, but rather we were all part of the decisions and itineraries. Ownership, ownership, ownership!

You have been to India several times before and know how challenging it can be for any traveler. Did you prepare the girls for anything specific?

Before we left, we explained about the poverty and some of the sad things they would see. I knew it would be upsetting for them to see the beggars and get inundated with people asking for money. I also knew it would be just as upsetting for them to have to see their dad turn away people asking for help, as we always try to give to people on the street here. So, we sat down and researched charities that feed the hungry in India, and made a donation before we left. We explained that it was impossible to help all the people who were going to ask for money, but we could do a donation beforehand that would likely help more people. That made them feel better about shunning beggars, knowing we had helped already.

What did they most enjoy about this adventure?

We had them pay for things as we went through the country . . . buy-in! They loved using the money and again, felt the ownership rather than feeling like they are just along for the ride. We brought home rupee notes and coins for all their classmates. They loved that!

The challenge of single-parent travel

While reflecting on a recent trip to Peru with her 13-year old daughter and 15-year old son, Claire explains how surprised she was by how their journey was tinged with a mild tension that was absent when her husband was with them. They had travelled extensively as a family over the years, but on this trip Claire was riding solo. *The kids were noticeably more cautious about venturing out in the evening or joining the New Year's Eve crowds. They thought I was being reckless in some of the decisions I was making, when in fact I was just acting like I normally did.*

Whether there was any actual cause for concern was unclear, but she thought it important to heed the kids' feelings. *Single-parents traveling with their kids to unfamiliar places might want to spend a little extra time planning things through, like when choosing a guide they feel comfortable with. I would spend more time discussing in advance our expectations for the trip, possible limitations and what we might encounter. My kids want to know the lay of the land.*

The anxious child

There is, no doubt, a difference between fussiness and anxiety. Any parent of an anxious child will tell you that. How to prepare such a child for what she might experience while travelling to a new and different place should be considered well in advance, rather than ignoring the signs and hoping that all turns out well. Your child's physician or psychologist may be able to provide advice about what can be done to cope before and during the trip. Moreover, you may have friends or family members who have had similar challenges to manage themselves and can provide some insight about what can be done. Several books on dealing with anxiety in children are available online and in bookstores.

ADAPTING MY STRIDE – Traveling with a Child with Special Needs

I offer here a few notes on how to accommodate the issues and challenges facing your special needs child while traveling. Sorry, I don't offer a long list of to-dos or suggestions. I don't think this accommodation is really so hard that one needs a long list. It's a lot more about reconsidering the type of trip you take than it is about adapting the trip you were planning. Do you get what I mean?

Let me clarify by telling a bit of my story and let me start by admitting that I've never been particularly good at adapting. Even for my own children. It's not easy for me to slow down, for example. When they were little, my children and I never strolled together. I'm sure you've seen mothers with their toddlers meandering about, exploring the world at the toddler's pace. You know how toddlers fall from object to object,: from flower to swing set to mud pie and back again. A 'walk' with a toddler may take hours, but you never really go anywhere. Unfortunately, my children never got to meander. I just kinda dragged them after me.

Unfortunately (?,) as my children grew older I found I did have to adapt somewhat- not so much to their speed but to their - or rather my son's - style and personality. My son has autism. His autism is by no means profound. DS has been mainstreamed without special supports since Grade 1. But then again, it isn't mild either. It's real autism. But whatever . . . DS has his capabilities and his challenges and he has a right, like any child with special needs, to have those challenges accommodated.

And, so we work to accommodate them.

But we live overseas. My husband, DS's dad, is Canadian. I'm American. His sister was adopted from Indonesia. DS was actually born in France but has been raised in Singapore and, more recently, in the Middle East. So, he has obviously traveled. To be an expatriate is, almost by definition, to travel.

But our travels have been different, perhaps, from those of other expats. They've been constrained by what DS could and couldn't do. I remember years ago having a girl friend who had a child that she could throw in the backpack. From the time the baby was 3 months old, he and his parents were exploring the developing world: cycling in Vietnam, backpacking in Laos, river rafting in Malaysia.

I was so jealous. Those were not our trips. Ours were mundane - touristy hotels on the beach. We needed trips that allowed us to maintain a routine similar to that at home - with similar food, similar activities, the same comforts and sensations. At these resorts, DS could play happily in the surf for hours and then spend a similar amount of time, with equal joy, in front of the television. No, I'm not complaining about 5-star hotel holidays. Our travels were fine and they worked for our family. But as DS grew I realized I was shortchanging both him and us. He/we needed to break out of the mold.

So . . . I began to think.

I didn't do anything formally . . . but I began to list the types of trips I would like to take and to think about why each one might work and why it might not.

I realized pretty quickly that there were a host of trips that would work. Interestingly, virtually all of them involved the great outdoors. Exploring the museums of Paris was out. Discovering the churches and cafes of Barcelona also wasn't the best. I knew he'd get bored and end up wanting only to spend time on his computer, which would mean sitting around the hotel room, which would mean too little exercise - and that would impact his ability to fall asleep. DS, like many kids with autism, ADHD, and other behavioral disorders needs to move his body a lot if he is to keep his mind calm and focused. So, whatever trip we were going to take needed to get him moving.

At first, I fell in love with the idea of farm stays or camping. But in truth, DS is very much a city boy and has no interest in mucking out the barn or pitching tents. Sadly. Canoeing or whitewater rafting was an idea. . . but that also involved some camping. Walking safaris are still on my to do list. And, skiing? Fantastic! Hiking? That works for us! Diving? Yup, that works. These are the kinds of trips that fit his needs.

So, for the past few years, all of our family holidays have been of this sort. We've hiked with the Boy Scouts in Nepal. We've taken a family trek around Land's End in Cornwall. We've gone reindeer sledding in Lapland and swished the slopes in Austria. As he's grown older, we've been able to motivate still more exercise and training with promises of, at some time, indulging in those walking safaris and hiking Kilimanjaro. And, we're getting really big on scuba diving trips, too. Diving can be physically challenging - which is exactly what we need. Another benefit comes with the serenity found in the deep. A day of diving isn't very different from a mindfulness meditation retreat. And, that's a good thing for a kid with autism.

DS is pretty fit now. And his improved physical health is without question impacting his emotional and psychological health and, ultimately, his ability to connect with others. Wow!

I suppose what I'm saying is that these trips with a special needs child can and probably will be one of the great gifts you ever give your child. If constructed well, they'll stimulate all sorts of healing. And, I swear, they won't be hard to manage. You'll simply need to invest some thought on his/her talents and needs. Rethink

> the type of trip you're going to take instead of trying to 'accommodate' him or her on the trip you think you ought to take.
>
> The world's a big place. There's no question that you can find the perfect experience for your family. Just think through who he or she is and start with that.
>
> - Sarah

Keeping plans under your hat

Despite the above advice about including your child in the planning process, there have been occasions when we've opted to keep our plans from the kids until *the time was just right*. When they asked for details, we provided an underwhelming summary. In this way, they couldn't hold us to the plan if things did not pan out, and they were happily surprised when things were not as mundane or miserable as they were led to believe. (Which was always!)

Sometimes we need to walk a fine line, particularly with our daughter. Once she learns something she likes the sound of, like an opportunity to play with animals or to go cliff diving, she will not let the idea drop. This can be frustrating when Sam and I decide to change our plans. Nagging and sulking is to be avoided at all costs when living cheek by jowl with one another 24-hours a day.

When we left Saigon for southern Vietnam, I told the kids we were going to *live rough* in a grass shack. That's all I said. Their minds raced toward something rather horrific, which was fine with me. When we arrived at our secluded compound to find two mangy but welcoming dogs at the entrance, who led us down a long path toward a collection of charming grass huts with hammocks, surrounded by palm and banana trees, Scout declared *This isn't rough! I want to stay here for the rest of the trip!* I knew then we had made the right decision to set low expectations for a higher payoff.

YOU DON'T NEED TO PAY FOUR-STAR PRICES FOR A PRICELESS EXPERIENCE.
MEKONG DELTA, VIETNAM

It's hard for most of us to keep focused on where we are in time and place, even when luxuriating in a tropical paradise or in the middle of a rock concert in Central Park. Our minds drift to the past or future, rather than hold us in *the now*. That is another reason why I sometimes limit how much I delve into the specifics of our travel plans – I want the kids to remain present where they are and to enjoy the moment rather than retreat into their imaginings of what lay ahead.

During our 10-day drive from Houston to Boston, the kids knew of our intentions to visit the National Civil Rights Museum and Al Green's gospel church in Memphis. I described how we would explore a part of West Virginia where our ancestors had lived from the 1600's, and what we might see in Amish Country, Pennsylvania. What I didn't mention was that we were also going to fit in a day at the Dollywood amusement park in the Smokey Mountains. If I had, all other experiences would have been overshadowed by their excitement about the forthcoming rollercoasters. We announced the news only the night before, after the kids had already enjoyed their visit to Elvis' Graceland, and witnessed a solar eclipse that we just happened to be perfectly situated for, in central Tennessee.

MANAGE ENERGY

Erica suggests that kids' energy levels need to be managed carefully for a holiday to run smoothly.

I have two middle school-aged boys and have always had to take their energy levels into account when planning trips. I suggest scheduling physical activity into each day. If a museum is planned for the morning, make sure that the rest of the day is spent doing something active – a hike or long walk, swimming, or even wrestling with their dad.

These days we are choosing holidays that center around outdoor activities, like skiing and fishing.

MIDDLE & HIGH SCHOOLERS

The main concern I hear raised by parents planning to take their teens on a family gap year tour is that they'll miss their friends. *It's true!* says Vivian, mother of two middle schoolers and a high schooler. *Middle schoolers, particularly those who have gone to school with the same kids since they were in kindergarten, worry that the social order will change in their absence. They're afraid that they will miss a lot with their friends, and won't be able to pick up where they left off. Parents need to think about it. Not every child can handle it.*

For parents who see this as a serious hurdle to their gap year plans, Vivian suggests *Maybe don't plan to go for quite so long. Summer holidays are long. Go for those eight-plus weeks, but get the kids back in time for the beginning of the new school year.*

This idea reminded me of Sam's colleague who chose to break his 12-month sabbatical into three four-month-long unpaid summer vacations, which he used over consecutive years. This allowed plenty of time with his kids during the most pleasant months of the year.

Vivian continues, *Elementary is easier. Homeschooling is easier for them. The transition back is easier.*

And what about high schoolers? I ask.

It's less an issue for high school kids who want something different, and are willing to try new things.

THE POWER OF MUSIC

Vivian suggests encouraging teens to bring their own music with them. A massive playlist helps teens feel connected to their community.

Parents might indeed want to keep these concerns in mind as they begin their travel planning, although they were actually not issues for our kids, and I can think of a couple of reasons why. Firstly, our kids had already attended international schools for most of their lives. In those institutions, kids came and went regularly, so relationships were built quickly, but they were not expected to last forever. Saying goodbye to friends was a normal part of their lives . . . as was saying hello to new ones.

Secondly, our kids had enough experience to know that they would meet people on the road. It didn't occur to either of them that their social lives began and ended at the school they were attending. Everywhere we visited, and with everything we did, the kids came across people to talk to and have fun with. They swam and collected shells with kids on beaches in the Philippines, and spent evenings in Africa playing interactive games with older teen volunteers from around the globe. They even played a local version of jacks with young San Bush children, who used dried kudu poop instead of metal jacks. How's that for a memory?

KIDS MAKE FRIENDS, WHEREEVER THEY GO.
TABLAS, PHILIPPINES.

North America - RV Communities

A friend of mine, Dan, describes how families touring North America by RV are building online communities who meet up with each other en route. This provides a chance for kids to make new friends, and their parents to enjoy adult conversation with likeminded travellers, in campsites around the continent. For more on this, see websites like:

- *Families on the Road*
- *Fulltime Families*

Social media keeps friends connected

Modern technology enabled us all to keep in contact with friends and family back home. While I updated my Facebook page with photos of our adventures, Sam exchanged occasional emails, and the kids, periodically, Skyped. Other travellers we met kept in touch through apps like *Viber, Whatsap, Snapchat* and *Instagram*, or whatever popular social media tool was being used by their communities.

If your kid doesn't already have one, you might consider allowing her to develop her own Facebook page for the journey. Or, create a family Facebook page that you can all share. The child can decorate the profile with photos from the trip and get her friends to join for regular updates.

Living off the grid

But before you take my advice about using social media to keep your kid connected to friends back home, there is another perspective to consider. Encouraging your child to rely on social media too much may not be the best option for him or your family, and may actually defeat some of the purpose of getting away from it all.

Would it be a genuine hardship for your child to leave his mobile phone at home while he explored the world with his family? Imagine enjoying hours of time together when every family member is truly present in the places you're in, soaking up the atmosphere, living in that moment, engrossed in face-to-face conversations, without the distraction of digital devices.

Sure, there might be some initial emotional withdrawal, even for *you*. But would it last? Only you can answer that for your family but, from our experience, I know that limiting access to the news, checking emails only occasionally, and sending few text messages felt like a modern-day liberation.

5 TAKE-AWAYS

1. Travelling pregnant is doable for many women. Be prepared to get around at a slightly slower pace, be sure to follow your doctor's instructions, take care to choose foods wisely and have a plan in case of emergency.

2. Traveling with a toddler usually requires adjustments to ambitious travel plans. Keep in mind activity levels, nap times and allowances for outside play. Babies and toddlers also require extra equipment – diapers, bottles, car seats, toys, buggies - so plan cleverly to minimize the weight.

3. A child generally grows more resilient and adventurous as she experiences new and varied things. As the parent, keep in mind that your own attitudes about differences and discomforts can influence your child's responses.

4. If your middle or high schooler is resistant to your travel plans because he's going to miss his friends, create opportunities to meet other kids on the road, and develop strategies for keeping him in touch with his friends back home. At the same time, weigh the pros and cons of your child depending too much on social media, as it may turn out to be an unwelcome distraction from your vacation.

5. Inviting a child's input in travel planning is widely considered a great way to make her enthusiastic about the trip, and to counter some of the anxiety she might be feeling. That said, depending on the nature of your child, there may be times when keeping plans under your hat may help keep things running smoothly.

PART B
LOGISTICS

Chapter 6

Building Your Itinerary

Now that you have had a glimpse into some travel options available to families, it's time to create an itinerary that will work for you. For this I suggest a straightforward process of brainstorming, researching and prioritizing.

AN ITINERARY PLANNING PROCESS

a. Brainstorm the possibilities

We brainstormed a long list of dream locations and activities, many of which came from scrolling through travel magazines and websites, conversations with well-travelled family and friends, books, and from our own earlier travel experiences.

b. Research

Once we had a general idea of regions that appealed to us, we began to consider the specifics – climate, activities and costs. Over the years we have built quite a library of *Lonely Planet* guides from which to gather intelligence about the countries we plan to visit. We have found that the consistently high-quality information in these books can push the planning process into full swing.

We also rely on *TripAdvisor* for ideas and travellers' reviews. Said to be the world's largest travel website, it provides an extraordinary range of travel advice about almost anything from grass bungalows in Vietnam and caving adventures in New Zealand, personal tour guides in Rome, to truck rentals in Namibia and mountain village retreats in remote Laos.

c. Identify the must do's

New Zealand topped this list for us as Sam had long wanted to take our family on a camper van tour through the country where he was born and raised. As February tends to have the best summertime weather in New Zealand, we built the entire gap year itinerary around our being there for that month.

Another place we had to include was France, where our ancient summer house had an almost endless list of repairs and renovations to be worked on. My engineer father agreed to direct some of the work on condition that we avoid the height of the French summer heat. This meant that we needed to arrive by May, at the latest.

SAM, SCOUT & MY BROTHER, MICHAEL, WORKING ON HOUSE RENOVATIONS. FRANCE

d. *Identify the really want to do's*

Sam and I had dreamed of going to Africa for years. He was most attracted to the idea of seeing the wildlife, whereas my thoughts drifted to doing some kind of humanitarian work with children and women. For Scout, working hands-on with monkeys in South Africa topped her list. She and I discovered the location during a rainy day of web surfing. Its website showed images of volunteers handling, feeding and even sleeping with baby vervet monkeys. To our 12-year old daughter, it looked like paradise.

MONKEY HEAVEN,
SOUTH AFRICA

Declan's priority was to return for a short visit to Singapore where we had lived for several happy years, and then head to a South-East Asian beach. Sam and Scout were keen to learn how to kite surf on the island of Boracay, Philippines, after hearing my brother rave about it. I was happy to give it a try, and was particularly keen to relax in a tropical paradise where we could enjoy the best mangos in the world. So, Boracay it was!

e. Prioritize

Narrowing our list down to a handful of locations and activities was essentially a process of elimination.

DESPITE ALL OUR EFFORTS, SCOUT WAS THE ONLY ONE WHO ACTUALLY MASTERED KITE SURFING.
BORACAY, PHILIPPINES

What is most important to us given our time and budget?

Beyond costs and schedules, there were other factors that influenced our priorities. Given that we were travelling with the kids, some locations in North Africa and the Middle East that Sam and I had longed to visit were scratched off the list due to safety concerns at the time. Mongolia was removed because the best travel months in that country – May to July – clashed with our plans to be in France. Going to South America would have added a layer of complication to an already ambitious flight schedule. *Another time!*

f. Group & Organize

Our final step before booking the flights was to work out how to use our time most wisely, by mapping out the itinerary according to geographic location and climate, and then where we wanted to be on specific dates.

Our final plan had us head straight to South-East Asia, then down to New Zealand, back north to the Philippines, then to Africa, and finally, Europe.

Our chosen locations and dates were forwarded to our around-the-world travel agent (See Chapter 7: *Getting There & Around*) who came up with a plan, including suggested airlines. With a few modifications here and there, our itinerary was confirmed, booked and paid for. Some changes were made en route, but by-and-large we stuck with the original plan.

KEEPING YOUR ITINERARY ORGANIZED

It is important to consider how you will keep track of your itinerary given the number of dates, locations, confirmation and booking numbers you will need while you're on the road. My personal preference is to create a simple table with enough space for the necessary information, rather than relying on a pre-made digital tool. During the tour, I kept the table on my desktop for easy retrieval and regular updates, backed up on iCloud.

I expect that there are sophisticated, perhaps more user-friendly, digital tools out there that might meet your needs better, but I don't know what they are. For now, I just want to raise your awareness about the types of information you may want to keep track of, such as: Arrival dates and times, accommodation booking details, flight numbers, contact details, reference numbers and special instructions. My working document looked something like this:

DATE	TRANSPORTATION	ACCOMMODATION	MISCELLANEOUS
Feb 3	S'pore to Auckland Singapore Airlines Flight SG1234 Dep. 13:40PM Arr. 5:05am (+1 day) Confirmation: P67HF1		
Feb 4		Otahuhu Travel Lodge 123 Carson Bld. Tel: 123 45 6789 (reservation – 2 nights)	Car pick-up Auckland Airport Cheap Car Rentals Confirmation #: 12344 6:00AM
Feb 5			Booked – tickets to Wet Hot Beauties 8:00PM at Victoria Theatre Pick up tickets at door
Feb 6	Auckland to Wellington Flight NZ4566 Dep. 6:30am, Arr. 8:00am Confirmation: H7H5H6	Pete and Ady's House 4859 Waikenae Ave. Tel: 278-283-4854 (4 nights)	Drop off car at Auckland airport by 5:00am ----- Camper pick-up at Camper Vans R'Us 2345 Pete Street, Wellington Tel: 786 432 8375 7:30am Confirmation number: 178362Y (deposit of 30% paid)
Feb 7			Booked - tour of Smith Farm Ask Judy for details.

5 TAKE-AWAYS

1. Begin by brainstorming your travel dreams. Invite ideas from the whole family. *Don't hold back!*

2. Research options, costs, climates, schedules and other details that will help you narrow down your list.

3. Prioritize according to what you *must* do and would *like* to do, and how it will fit with your schedule and budget.

4. Organize your choices according to region to help manage your flight schedule and luggage requirements to specific climates. (More on that in Chapter 9: *Pack Your Bags.*)

5. Keep track of your itinerary and reservations on a single document for easy reference and updates. Keep a backup on a memory stick or in the Cloud.

Chapter 7
Getting There & Around

Accommodation and flights are likely to compete for the top spot on your expenses' list. Here are some lessons and tricks we have learnt over the years that might help you manage those costs.

PLANES

Around-the-World Flights vs. Frequent-Flyer Miles

As the idea of our family gap year began to blossom, we discussed using some of our air miles accumulated over the years to buy around–the-world-tickets. After careful examination, however, it became clear that that would have been an unwise use of our points. Here's why:

- Around-the-world tickets through alliance programs usually require passengers to travel in a single direction – i.e. east to west. Our ideal itinerary, however, had us flying around in different directions. We did not want to be dictated to by this restriction.

- More significantly, and much to our surprise, the cost of the points' tickets would have been prohibitively high. The tax and service fees were, quite frankly, extortionate. They alone would have cost us *twice* what we ended up paying for our around-the-world tickets organized through a specialist agent, plus we would have used up a huge chunk of our points in the process.

In the end, we purchased reasonably priced tickets through the online specialist agent **Air Treks**, which took us to five central locations on four continents. We then applied our frequent-flyer points to regional flights, as described below:

AROUND-THE-WORLD TICKET

Houston — Singapore — Auckland — Manila — Johannesburg — Toulouse — Houston

AROUND-THE-WORLD
+ regional frequent-flyer points' flights

Houston — Singapore – *Bangkok, Luang Prabang, Ho Chi Minh* – Auckland — Manila – *Boracay* — Johannesburg – *Hoedspruit, Windhoek, Victoria Falls* — Toulouse – *London* — Houston

Without meaning to sound too enthusiastic about Air Treks' customer service, it genuinely was an excellent experience working with them on our family's itinerary. The interactive website enabled us to begin exploring routing options (and get a sense of prices) with ease, before working one-on-one with an agent. We enjoyed personalized attention during the planning process and throughout the tour. All questions and flight changes were responded to quickly and knowledgably.

More thoughts about frequent-flyer miles

All four family members have long been members of frequent-flyer points' programs, which has helped us save a considerable amount of money over the years. The following suggestions come from years of our own trials and errors.

- Most airlines today belong to a cooperative network of airlines. As a member, you collect points on flights you take on any of the airlines in the group. These points can then be redeemed for future flights. You can also use your points toward hotel and car rental chains, amongst other things.

  To accumulate points, join a carrier network or two that you expect to use often. Try to use those airlines whenever you fly, within reason. Of course, there will be times when you find good discounted flights on other carriers. Take them! Ultimately, your goal is to save money.

  I suggest that you explore airline websites to learn who they are partnered with, as well as the membership benefits you'll receive. Currently, the largest airline networks are:

  - Star Alliance
  - One World
  - Sky Team

- There are several easy-to-find websites that offer free advice about how best to collect and utilize your frequent-flyer points. I suggest that you take a look at a few of these before using your points, as these sites are updated regularly and will touch on current issues and benefits. Begin your search with:
  - thepointsguy.com
  - thepennyhorder.com/travel-hacking-blogs

In addition to gaining points by flying on specific airlines, you can earn points simply by using partner credit cards. We have chosen credit cards specifically because they offer attractive sign-on bonuses – 30,000 to 50,000 points – that can be used toward travel expenses. Purchases on these cards earn you points, as well. Note that we have no qualms about closing a credit card account as soon we've used the sign-on points for flights.

Credit card programs change regularly so I recommend comparison shopping before signing up. The following websites provide helpful information about travel-oriented credit cards on the market:
  - creditcards.com/compare/Airline-offers
  - creditkarma.com/AirineMiles/creditcards
  - nerdwallet.com/creditcards/AirlinePoints

- Points are not automatically earned on all flights within the network. Conditions vary according to the airline, specific flight class and price paid for the ticket.

On previous flights between Asia and Europe, for example, I made the mistake of flying on two European airlines in the Star Alliance group, which we were members of at the time.

I wrongly assumed that by choosing those airlines I would automatically earn points on those long-haul flights. It was only after the trips, when I checked my account, that I learnt that the tickets had not earn us any points because of the class I had chosen. Had I known that, I would have chosen to fly on less expensive airlines. Thus, I recommend that if points are important to you, check with the airline in advance to confirm that your chosen flight will earn you points.

- Be aware that tax and service fees add up, and can significantly reduce the value of your points.

  From our experience, flights in and out of Europe can come with particularly high tax and service fees, while using up large chunks of valuable points. As a result, we think twice before using our points on flights to those destinations and instead reserve them for regional flights in Asia and North America, where the fees and taxes are more reasonable.

- There are black-out periods, often during the summer, Christmas and Thanksgiving, when airlines limit the number of points-seats available. For this reason, I recommend that you book well in advance for those periods, or plan to use the points during less popular seasons.

- In theory, you should be able to use points earned on one airline to buy flights on partner airlines, although it's not always that straight forward. Airlines generally reserve a limited number of seats that can be purchased with partner airline points. For this reason, it is wise to book these seats well in advance.

- Your points can be used to purchase tickets for your friends and family.

FINDING CHEAP AIR TICKETS

Our family friend, Billy, has a knack for finding great deals on flights.

It's simple! he explains. *Just start by signing up for several websites that promote services for finding cheap flights. I like **SmarterTravel**, which allows me to indicate routes I'm interested in and then they send emails with different prices for those. **Travel Zoo** and **Secret Flying** provide similar services.*

***Kayak Explorer** is good because it allows me to input how much I'm willing to pay for flights during a specific period – i.e. $500 per person in April – and it then sends me a list of destination options.*

Have you heard of Error Fares?

Yes. These cheap fares are caused by computer glitches. Flights are advertised well below their intended prices and if you book quickly, before the airline spots the mistake, they'll usually honor the price.

Have you ever used an Error Fare?

Yes. Recently we purchased return tickets between Houston and Amsterdam for an astonishing $249 per person, which is close to a quarter of the usual price. We had to fly via Mexico City, which added about four hours to the flight, but it saved us thousands of dollars in the process. Error Fares are explained on many travel websites.

TRAINS

Overland train travel has its benefits – the most obvious being that it allows passengers to view the countryside pass by. It can also be a convenient and cost-effective way to get around.

Sam and I took our first train trip together years ago in Vietnam, from Hanoi towards Sapa, in the northern mountains overlapping the Chinese border. It was only when we got on the train that we realized it was the high-end *Victoria Express Train*, reminiscent of the legendary Orient Express, including private berths decked out with wood paneling, elegant décor, fine linens and silverware. The train moved slowly through the mountains allowing plenty of time to soak in the atmosphere. Quite frankly, it was wonderful!

In Japan, train travel is a must. It is how the average Japanese get around quickly and efficiently. Local trains stop more frequently, are less expensive, and give travellers a sense of Japanese daily life. For long distance travel, our family prefers to travel by *Shinkansen* or *bullet train*, which is entirely comfortable and, as far as we've experienced, always on time. Our kids enjoy purchasing quintessentially Japanese snacks on board, like dried octopus and *onigiri* (rice and fish wrapped in seaweed), while we fly along the tracks. The highlight of our kids' journeys is the sight of the cart ladies who invariably turn, just as they are about the leave the carriage, and bow.

To find several websites that provide information about routings, prices, special passes and discounts on Japanese trains, type in *Japan Rail*.

Another memorable train trip we took was in China when the kids were 10 and 11 years old. Sam and I both feel that kids should not be sheltered from less luxurious travel, so part of our multi-hour journey from Pingyao to Datong, and finally Beijing, included a few hours soaking up the ambience of third-class *Hard Seat*. The carriages were crowded, the wooden seats were indeed hard, the windows would not open so we choked on cigarette smoke exhaled by our fellow passengers despite the 'no smoking' signs, and the smell of the overflowing toilets wafted along the aisles, as we sat with our shirts clutched over our faces.

Was it an enjoyable experience? No, not at the time, but we kept our humor about us and it was far more memorable than the following journey which was comparable to a luxurious Japanese train. To this day we enjoy laughing about that experience on those hard seats.

Three other train trips remain on our family's To Do list, starting with the Beijing to Lhasa, Tibet journey that takes passengers through some of the most spectacular Himalayan landscape. It's a two-day trek, plus a two or three-day stop mid-level (at an altitude of around 7,000 feet) to acclimate to the higher altitude. Another option to the north is the Trans-Mongolian Railway journey that follows an ancient caravan route from China to Russia. It connects Ulan-Ude, on the Trans-Baikal railway in Russia, with the Chinese city of Jining, via Ulaanbaatar in Mongolia. Long-time friends of ours, Isabelle and Tim, chose the most ambitious train trip of all, the 9,289 kilometer (5,772 mile) Trans-Siberian rail journey from Moscow to Vladivostok, with connecting routes to Mongolia and China. It is the longest railway line in the world. It may be a slow way to cover the world's largest continent, but what a fascinating view!

Eurail

Although flying can be more efficient and, with so many discount airlines today, cost-effective, there is something special about train travel in Europe. My mother discovered the Eurail pass back in the 1980s and it soon became our family's favourite way to travel. We especially enjoyed the liberty of walking into the train station in Geneva or Florence or Paris only to ask ourselves *Shall we go to Vienna today or Monte Carlo?* The freedom to choose on a whim was half the fun!

Passes can only be purchased outside of Europe – see **Eurail.com** - and are priced according to class and the length of time you plan to use them, from a few days to a number of weeks. Many trains include sleeping berths for overnight trips, which can help reduce your accommodation costs.

From my experience, spontaneous train travel is best enjoyed during lower season periods, when seats do not need to be reserved in advance, and hotels and B&Bs are more likely to have rooms available wherever you decide to disembark.

CARS

These days we rent cars for most of our vacations – be it in Europe, New Zealand, North America, Australia and even Namibia – because of the freedom they allow.

If you are considering the possibility of renting a vehicle during your gap year, here are some points to consider:

- In many countries, renting a car can be significantly less expensive than going by train or air, particularly when traveling with multiple people.

- The credit card you use to pay for your car rental may cover some, or all, of the insurance you'll need. This can save you a fair amount on the final bill.

- A special international driver's license seems to be a thing of the past. Your local driver's license should be accepted in most countries, by most car rental companies.

- To learn which side of the road is used in a country, simply go online and type in *Which side of the road,* followed by the country's name. There are several websites that can help with this.

- Note that cars with standard transmission are significantly more common in Europe than automatic, and they are less expensive to rent. If you are uncomfortable driving standard, you may want to do your research in advance to find out what your options are.

- There is normally an extra charge for a child's car seat, so you may choose to bring your own. Depending on how long you plan on renting the vehicle, it might even be worth purchasing a car seat in that location rather than paying the daily rental fee.

Comparison shop

It is wise to comparison shop before choosing a rental car, as prices can vary dramatically from one website to the next. These sites are just a few that help travelers find the best deals:

- Hotwire
- Argus Car Hire
- CheapTickets
- Orbitz
- Priceline

BIKING

Daniela explains that her family especially likes bikes. *We hired electric bikes to visit the ancient temples in Bagan, Myanmar; bicycles to tour the Via Apia just outside of Rome (with frequent stops for photos, water, and catacombs); mountain bikes in Bali (from the top of a volcano crater near Mt Agung to Ubud, with frequent stops to visit local villages, rice fields, temples). We also completed a bike tour of Washington D.C., Beijing in China, Luang Prabang in Laos, Guilin and around the city wall in Xi'an, China.*

MOPED & MOTORBIKE

Motorbikes and mopeds are commonly available for rent in South-East Asia. We've used them in Thailand, Indonesia, Vietnam and the Philippines. To be frank, they're *not* safe, so we haven't used them often with the kids. When we have, we were sure to wear helmets, drive cautiously, and limit ourselves to quiet roads with few other vehicles.

During our gap year, the four of us explored the rural hills in a remote area of Laos on the backs of two mopeds. We enjoyed viewing lush forests and dirt roads framed by rice fields, grass huts, grazing buffalo and smiling, waving children. And then we ran out of gas. Both bikes! Panic could have set in - *Where are we going to get gas out here? There are no gas stations!* - had we not done this before. We knew that in that tiny village we had driven through a couple of miles back, someone would be willing to sell us some fuel. And we were right. We found a little shop on the side of the road, selling a little of this and a little of that, including recycled water bottles full of enough gas to get us back to town.

A GAS STATION RURAL-LAOS STYLE.

JEN LIKES TO CRUISE

My friend, Jen, is a busy entrepreneur who works long hours and doesn't always get enough time with her three sons. Over the years she has worked out that a family cruise is the ideal remedy for her stressful life. She light-heartedly calls it *"adventure-lite."*

Why is your preferred family vacation on board a cruise ship?

When it's time for a holiday I need to relax, but I also enjoy visiting foreign ports. My kids can run around the ship freely while I put my feet up. Besides, I like to spend time with my elderly parents, and cruises are great for that. It's the ideal multi-generational holiday!

Aren't cruises expensive?

If you think about it, the price covers accommodation, transportation, meals (unlimited food, even for my ravenous teenage sons) and entertainment, while traveling to different ports. Even flights to the ship can be included in the price.

The fact that it's an all-inclusive package makes things much easier for me as a busy mother who doesn't have much time to plan vacations.

Do you have any suggestions for how parents can save money on a family cruise?

Never pay the asking price! Get on mailing lists of companies who deal with cruise ship discounts. Book well in advance. Also, gratuities can be expensive so to save money, look for deals that cover them.

Do your three boys enjoy cruise ship vacations?

Yes, they do. They enjoy the freedom to come and go as they please and to hang out with other kids on board.

It's important to check out the kids' entertainment options when doing your research. You'll find that there may be games rooms, dance and art classes, swimming pools, bowling alleys, Broadway-type shows and a lot more that kids enjoy.

Do you think cruises are good for all kids?

Personally, I prefer to take kids who are at least 10 years old so they can be given the freedom to entertain themselves. Younger kids need to be watched. Some cruises offer babysitting services but I prefer to keep the kids with me when they're younger.

Cruises might also be a great option for families with children with special needs as all of the entertainment and facilities are right there with you. Facilities are usually wheelchair friendly.

Do you have a dream cruise?

Yes, there are 180-day around-the-world cruises that look wonderful. What an easy and luxurious way to see the world!

BUSSES

If you want to get closer to, and a little bit more personal with, a population, I suggest giving local busses a try.

Years ago, when Sam and I were still very much traveling on the proverbial shoestring through China, we went by local bus from Baotou to Wudangzhao. It took us through local townships where people still lived in caves carved out of the rock, until we reached the remote Buddhist monastery we had come to see.

The journey was unexpectedly exotic and memorable, but perhaps what made it most entertaining was the chaos that ensued between the drivers and attendants of two buses who almost came to blows over who got to take the rich (in other words, over-paying) *wai guo ren* (foreigners). It was somewhat embarrassing to be the objects of such a show, and the other passengers couldn't help but glare at us when they realized their misfortune of having us on their bus. I think in the end a bit of money was exchanged to keep both parties happy, which, no doubt, was passed onto us in the form of a higher fare. (Probably a matter of a few cents, truth be told.) But in the end, it was an amusing story we'll always remember with a chuckle.

Similarly, Sam and I leapt onto a local bus travelling between Palembang and Bukittingi, Sumatra years ago. It seemed to stop at every possible bus stop along the road, which made it slow as well as hot and cramped. It was worth it, though, to be surrounded by warm and welcoming Indonesians, with whom we struggled to communicate through a combination of sign language and Bahasa Indonesia, which Sam had studied briefly at university. It was a wonderful opportunity to connect with local people.

Despite the cultural benefits of travelling by local bus, many countries today have Greyhound-standard buses to get around by. Of course, any industrialized country will have quality buses, but we have also seen them in Africa, China and Mexico. It's the comfortable option, if perhaps slightly less exotic than its local cousin.

BOATS

Travelling by boat up the Nam Ou River from Nong Khiaw to Muong Ngoy, Laos, was like taking local bus travel to the next level. The startlingly narrow motorized boat had passengers facing into the middle where our knees locked together. There was little room to adjust to make ourselves comfortable, but it was a joy just the same. Scout and Declan were quick to make friends with the other passengers, with whom we traded our exotic Lao snacks for other exotic Lao snacks.

The view from the river allowed us a special perspective of the villages we passed by. We saw children frolicking in the water while buffalo grazed along the shore. Buddhist monks in their bright saffron robes sped past in their motorboats, leaving us in their holy wakes. We so much preferred this unique mode of travel over the comfortable private Toyota van that transported us from Luang Prabang to the river port.

SPLASHES OF SAFFRON
NONG KHIAW, LAOS.

VARIETY IS THE SPICE

An adventure can be as much about the journey as the destination. Just like I would never recommend that you spend your nights in a series of hotel chains, so too would I not suggest that you stick with tried and tested modes of transportation. Risk getting closer to the places and people you have come to see by travelling alongside them. A passage on a noisy fishing boat between islands in Indonesia or the Philippines, can be an ideal opportunity to begin a conversation with local passengers. Branch out! Be open! Isn't that why you travel?

ON OUR WAY TO MEET OUR MONK MENTOR, IN THE BACK OF A PICK-UP TRUCK.
LAOS

5 TAKE-AWAYS

1. If you are considering multiple stops around the globe, an around-the-world ticket through a specialist agent might be your best option, in terms of cost and convenience.

2. Flyer miles are essentially travel dollars, so use them wisely. Comparison shop to work out which flights, at specific times, require the fewest points, with the lowest taxes and service fees. Several online sites provide useful advice on collecting and using points to your best advantage.

3. Renting a car or camper van can be the most cost effective and efficient way to transport families, although it can also limit your face-to-face interaction with local people. Be sure to comparison shop for the best price, and ask if your credit card covers insurance costs.

4. Trains, buses and boats can be a fun way to travel, while bringing you closer to local people.

5. Including a cruise on your journey might be a great option, particularly for families with members who appreciate (or require) comfort and convenience. It can be the ideal solution for a parent who has limited time to plan every detail of a journey, as the itinerary, accommodation, food and entertainment are all included. Discounted options can be found, so shop around.

Chapter 8

Where to Stay

It is entirely conceivable that your family could enjoy free, or considerably discounted, accommodation for the entirety of your gap year. The online services described below are used for short to long-term stays, and each has the added advantage of allowing families to enjoy a temporary home in locations of their dreams.

HOME SWAP

Has it ever occurred to you that someone living in the foothills of Tuscany might like to live in your home for a few weeks, while you stay in theirs? Would you be prepared to have a family stay in your house for a month, while you stayed in their holiday villa in Phuket, Thailand? These kinds of arrangements are being made by people every day through websites like **HomeExchange, Love Home Swap, Knok, International Vacation Home Exchange (IVHE)** and **Intervac**. They are like matchmaking services for homeowners.

I first experienced this kind of arrangement years ago when I stayed with a friend from Vancouver who arranged a six-week condo swap through HomeExchange.com with a couple in Versailles, France. As part of their arrangement, they agreed to share each other's cars, which added to the incredible cost savings they both enjoyed. I took the idea home with me to Beijing, and the following summer Sam and I arranged to swap homes with a family in Singapore. Rather than using the online service this time, we tapped into our connections to find a Singapore-based family interested in living in China for a few weeks. The arrangement worked out well.

Both of our families saved money on accommodation and enjoyed the use of each other's vehicles.

Perhaps you have Facebook friends, or friends of friends, who would be open to a holiday house swap. If not, why not give one of the online services a try?

Types of House Swaps

There are three types of home exchanges popular with travellers. The first is referred to as a *simultaneous* exchange, meaning that the two parties swap their homes at the same time. This is the arrangement I experienced in France and Singapore, as described above.

A *non-simultaneous* arrangement is for those who choose to swap at different times. For instance, Party A might make their beachside cottage available for the summer in exchange for the use of Party B's New York flat over the Christmas holidays.

The third type of exchange is commonly referred to as a *hospitality exchange*, whereby the parties act as hosts to each other in their homes. This might be an ideal arrangement for families keen to learn some of the language and local culture through the exchange.

Making it happen

Begin by researching the home exchange websites to work out which provides the services, membership arrangements and fees you're most comfortable with. Once registered, you're free to read through the social-media vetting and recommendations that go with the home you're interested in swapping for.

Next, contact the other party, explain your interest in their place, as well as the dates you are considering. If interested, the other party reads what's written about you and your home on the website to see if it's a suitable match. There may be some further back and forth to work out the arrangements – for instance, if you will also be exchanging vehicles or intend to engage cleaning services.

Once all is agreed, follow the instructions provided by your specific website to finalize the arrangement.

HOUSESITTING

Another attractive option is housesitting in lieu of rent. Homeowners and travellers from around the world register on websites like **trustedhousesitters.com** to make connections. We used the service during our gap year to have our house and dogs cared for in our absence. (I give a full description of the arrangement in Chapter 10: *Managing the Home Front*.) It turned out to be an excellent outcome for all parties concerned. The house sitters got to enjoyed living in Houston for a few months, and we saved thousands of dollars in dog sitting and house management fees.

PRIVATE RENTAL

Like many travellers today, we regularly turn to websites like **Airbnb** and **HomeAway** to find accommodation. These sites enable private house and condo owners to advertise their places for rent for days to months. We find that this is often the best way to get two or more rooms for our family of four, without paying for two expensive hotel rooms. It also means that we can use the kitchen facilities to reduce eating costs.

Scanning through the sites will give you a long list of unique travel ideas. How does staying in a treehouse in Vermont sound? What about spending a few weeks living out of a villa in Sri Lanka? Or a ski-in/ski-out cabin close to the slopes? We have found these and other wonderful options through these sites. At the time of writing, we actually have an autumn weekend in a windmill booked on Cape Cod, Massachusetts. What fun!

Similarly, **SabbaticalHomes.com** and **sabbatical.com** match academics on term or multi-term sabbaticals with travellers open to renting, swapping or housesitting.

HOTELS & B&Bs

Staying in a hotel or bed-and-breakfast is the most obvious accommodation option chosen by travellers. Finding the right one for you may require some research and comparison shopping.

In recent years, helpful websites like **Kayak** and **Trivago** have popped up to assist travelers in comparing hotel prices advertised on various websites. The differences can be significant, so take the time to do your research.

We also use specialist B&B websites like **Bedandbreakfast.com**.

Once again, it's wise not to limit your search to my recommended sites. It seems that every day new, helpful travel sites are being launched.

OUR SECOND HOME ON THE MEKONG DELTA.
VIETNAM

5 TAKE-AWAYS

1. Home swapping enables families to temporarily trade houses or apartments to enjoy living like locals, do in different parts of the world. Simultaneous, non-simultaneous and hospitality exchanges are three popular home swap options.

2. Through websites like trustedhousesitters.com, families arrange to watch people's homes (and often their pets) in exchange for free accommodation. On the flipside, families enjoy the peace of mind of having their homes and pets watched for free, while they travel.

3. Rather than staying in a traditional hotel or B&B, your family can rent a house directly from a homeowner through websites like AirBnB. Added benefits might include greater space than you would get from a standard hotel room, the use of a kitchen, more affordable prices and opportunities to stay in quirky options like boathouses, cabins and treehouses.

4. Faculty members on short to long-term leave advertise their homes for rent or housesit through websites like Sabbatical.com. Furnished homes listed on these sites are often priced lower than standard rentals.

5. If you do choose to use a hotel or B&B for part or all of your gap year, comparison shop through internet sites like Kayak and Trivago, set up to allow comparison price shopping for the same properties offered on multiple websites.

Chapter 9

Pack Your Bags

Many stressful moments of my travel life have been spent worrying that I have forgotten something, just as I board a plane. At such times, it's comforting to remember that all one actually needs is a passport and a credit card – everything else can be got along the way.

But who wants to spend travel money or time shopping for things that could have easily been packed? This chapter is dedicated to those of you who do *not* want to forget anything you and your family might need as you head off on your gap year travels.

THE ART OF PACKING

Packing right for your long voyage is a chore that should not be overlooked. There's nothing enjoyable about trying to manage several bulky bags while navigating through a crowded, unfamiliar city. Climbing on and off trains, through rain or snow, into a rickshaw or off the back of a truck with heavy luggage in hand can put a real damper on any family's fun. The same can be said for arriving somewhere to realize you left that much-needed warm jacket in your closet at home, or did not think to bring a back-up phone charger *just in case*.

Travel light

As our family's official travel planner, my challenge has always been to anticipate everything we might need for the trip, and then reduce it down to what you *really* need. It's harder than it sounds.

Limiting what we pack can save a surprising amount of time otherwise spent hunting for things while on the road. This may not be an obvious benefit to single or fastidious travellers but, in truth, my kids and husband, and probably I, do not always put things back where they were found. Instead, there's a lot of grabbing and stuffing into any bag as we head off to our next destination, only to be left with a lot of pulling out and rummaging at the other end. Huge amounts of time can be lost searching for your sunglasses, that missing sock, the sunscreen or a Kindle. For those likely to suffer through this, I highly recommend that you scale way back on what you bring with you.

Admittedly, by the time we set off on our gap year we had grown much better about stuffing without thinking. Crucial items had their special places in specific bags, which made things run far more efficiently, we lost less stuff and saved time. Oh, and it probably led to a bit less bickering, to boot.

Our Packing Process

Here is a packing process that has worked for us over the years. Let me begin by saying that the earlier the process begins the better because it takes time to get things just right.

1. Brainstorm all the environments, and most importantly climates, you are expecting to visit.

    - *Will we be in a damp tropical rainforest?*

    - *What day and nighttime temperatures can we expect in the desert?*

    - *Do we plan on camping in a mosquito-infested forest?*

    - *Do we expect to attend events that will require formal or semi-formal attire?*

    - *Will we be going swimming?*

144

2. Go online to research the temperatures and rainfall (or snowfall) you should expect at each location at the time of year you plan to be there.

3. Write up packing lists for each family member, and put these in a single document. Some items will fall into the "Family" column, which covers things to be shared, like shampoo.

   Note that I usually keep this page as a working document on my desktop for days or weeks leading up to the trip, adding and deleting items as our plans evolve. I then bring this list on the trip to keep track of things.

Sam	Declan	Scout	Taryn	Family
4 t-shirts	4 t-shirts	3 t-shirts	3 t-shirts	2 computer chargers
1 jeans	1 plaid shirt	2 sweatshirts	1 sweater	camera tripod
2 shorts	1 rain poncho	1 skirt	1 cotton dress	shampoo

4. Search through your belongings to work out what you already have and place them in an allocated spot.

   Make certain that the kids' clothes fit. After sitting in a closet for a few months, kids' pants and bathing suits have the most amazing way of growing too small for their owners. Ask yourself, *Will those shoes still fit her in two months' time?*

5. Buy, borrow or steal whatever else you need.

6. Checked-in bags don't always make it to your destination at the same time as you do, so pack your irreplaceable valuables, money, credit cards, passports, medications, computers, iPads, memory sticks containing important documents, cameras and phones in your carry-on luggage. If you wear glasses, keep at least one pair in a separate carry-on.

7. Pack the rest of your bags in a logical order so that everything can be found easily by every member of the family.

PACKING TIPS & TRICKS

Thoughts on clothes:

- Remember that you can find cheap t-shirts and other clothing items virtually anywhere in the world, so don't bother bringing enough for your entire trip. Expect to throw things out and replace them along the way. This also goes for toothpaste and other toiletries that can be found anywhere, even in developing countries.

- Since we're not that fussy, we find that shampoo works well enough as a substitute for laundry soap. Otherwise, a zip-locked bag of laundry soap can be refilled along the way. In many developing countries, we arrange to have our clothes washed by local laundry services at reasonable prices.

- Leave some space for purchases made along the way, but not too much.

    Plan to send your souvenirs to a designated address back home so you don't have to carry them around with you. If you are uncomfortable about using the local postal service, FedEx, DHL and UPS can be found almost anywhere.

- Shoes and bras that fit *Western* sizes are not always readily available in other countries. If you are generally bigger (or smaller) than the locals, bring what you need with you for the entirety of the trip.

- Whenever possible, work out how a single clothing item can be used for more than one purpose. For instance, for years I have packed a sarong for every trip because it can be used as a wrap to dress up an outfit and to keep warm with, around my waist as a skirt in casual locations, to cover up for entering religious sites, and as an ad hoc picnic or beach blanket.

- Stretch your wardrobe by matching each pair of shorts and pants with all your t-shirts, shirts, sweaters and outer layers.

- Pack layers that can be put on and taken off as the weather dictates. For instance, start with a light t-shirt, then add a buttoned shirt, a light sweater or sweatshirt, a warm/water resistant jacket, and finally a rain poncho to cover everything.

- Bring along one light-weight dress-up option. Scout and I each had a skirt or light dress, and the guys had nice shirts that worked well with their khaki pants. For the locations we visited, even France, that was as formal as we needed to get. These clothes were also useful for getting into religious sites where modest dress was required. Also, don't choose a dress-up outfit that requires an entirely different pair of shoes.

- We found that a pair of travel sandals and closed-toe hiking shoes were all we needed for our feet. For myself, I made sure to choose an innocuous pair of beige sandals that looked fine for those few mildly dress-up occasions. We did buy cheap flip-flops on the beach in the Philippines that were thrown away when we left.

- Durable, light and easily compactible plastic rain ponchos are ideal for emergency rain weather.

- *Special note for travellers to Africa:* Wild animals are known to react aggressively to bright colors. Beiges and khaki greens are your safest bet.

IN OUR AFRICAN UNIFORM - BEIGE, BEIGE, KHAKI AND BEIGE – ALL DAY, EVERY DAY.
SOUTH AFRICA

Keeping things safe:

- Add something to the outside of your check-in bags to make them distinguishable from others', as it is easy to pick up someone else's bag at Baggage Claim by mistake. For years, we have used the cheap and easy system of tying colored yarn onto each of our checked bags.

- One mistake I will never make again is to bring only one pair of prescription glasses, after losing mine on our honeymoon. Since then I have made sure to pack at least two pairs of glasses and sunglasses, divided between different bags in case one is lost. I also keep my eye-glass prescription in the Cloud in case a pair needs to be made en route.

- Split important medications between different carry-on bags, in case one is lost. I also suggest keeping a copy of your prescriptions with you, or in the Cloud, in case replacement is necessary. Note that common brand-name pain relievers and over-the-counter medications can be purchased virtually anywhere in the world.

- Bring a compact travel first aid kit. During our world tour, we added a thermometer, additional acetaminophen, band aids and Tiger Balm for fevers. Our doctor prescribed broad-spectrum antibiotics to have on hand in case of emergency.
- Back up all trip photos, copies of important documents and homeschooling assignments on a thumb drive. Numbers and documents to be kept safe include:
  - Your itinerary plan, including reservation booking confirmations (flights, hotels and tours)
  - Passport numbers and passport photocopies
  - Frequent flyer numbers
  - Credit card details and bank phone numbers
  - Emergency phone numbers
  - Medical/dental insurance reference numbers and phone numbers
  - Photocopies of immunization cards

Other helpful hints:

- Hotels often lack adequate numbers of electrical sockets for charging several devices at one time – computers, Kindles, cameras, phones, iPads. Therefore, we bring along charger plugs that allow several devices to be charged from one socket at a time.
- While the devices are charging, wind the charger cables around the handles of your backpacks so they are not left behind.
- Having several good-sized, clear plastic cosmetic/travel bags helped us keep our toiletries and medications organized - one

for soaps and shampoos, another for medications, one for toothbrushes and toothpaste, and another for first aid items.

Managing luggage for specific regions

During the itinerary planning process, we grouped locations according to climate in order to reduce what we needed to bring. For instance, from our base in Singapore, we visited Vietnam, Thailand and Laos one after the other. Since they share a similar climate and culture we were able to scale down to a few clothing garments suitable for all three places. Those locations are generally hot and humid, and the travel culture is pretty casual – no need to waste valuable packing space on dress-up wear.

What we did not need for that leg was left in two duffle bags stored at our hotel in Singapore – since we had booked to return to the hotel, they were happy to store the bags for free. When we finished our time in Southeast Asia, we headed back to Singapore, exchanged some of the warm-weather clothing for fleeces, thick socks and sleeping bags, and headed for New Zealand. Once again, we left a duffle bag at the hotel containing our gear needed for Africa, which we picked up on our way through from the Philippines. Such is the benefit of having a central hub that you intend to fly in and out of more than once.

If it sounds like a workable solution for you, I suggest contacting your hotel in advance to make sure they will allow it.

Similarly, when travelling in Southern Africa we left our duffle bags in the Left Baggage facility in Johannesburg's O.R. Tambo International Airport. We were charged for this service, of course, but it was worth the luxury of not having to pack around unnecessary luggage while camping across Namibia.

Managing with small backpacks

By storing our large duffle bags in the two hubs – Singapore and Johannesburg - we were free to scale down to a carry-on sized backpack for each of us that comfortably sufficed for several weeks at a time. We each had our own *Osprey 46"* backpack, which was an ideal size designed with a front compartment for our computers and other homeschooling supplies.

LOST IN TRANSPORTATION

Tina writes:

Remember to check all seat pockets before disembarking the plane. Kids always leave things behind!

My response:

True! But it's not only kids who do that. Sam and I have lost more than one Kindle this way! Our new rule is – Nothing goes in the pocket in the seat in front of you. It must go straight back into the bag. I then loosely tie the strap of the bag around my leg.

Tina continues:

Count the luggage before leaving the airport. The number of times we have accidentally left a bag behind is ridiculous.

My response:

We now use our phones to photograph our bags before checking them in, in case they get lost.

Tina continues:

Check that the kids have everything back in their daypacks before leaving the airport. My kids always unpack their day packs to get out activities while they wait for the luggage.

Benefits of carry-on size

Whenever possible, we carry our bags on flights with us rather than check them in. It saves us time at our destination, and we never worry about our bags being lost by the airline.

This lesson was learnt the hard way years ago when *all* of our check-in luggage missed a connecting flight in Paris. It took 11 stressful days for the bags to finally reach us, by which point we had already bought new clothes and supplies. Perhaps the worst part was that some of our important medications were in those bags - a mistake we have been careful not to repeat.

Day Bags

During the day, we each have our own day-bags to carry cameras, wallets, glasses and sunglasses. Declan's bag is usually big enough for the entertainment items described below.

My day bag, which also carries the family's passports, is a handy sling design that conveniently goes across my chest and opens in the front, allowing things to be retrieved easily and kept safe.

Don't forget entertainment!

Whenever travelling, we make sure to take light-weight entertainment items with us to pull out in restaurants and airports. Here are some examples:

- Pencils and pads for drawing
- *Yahtzee* pads and dice
- *Monopoly Card Deal*
- Trivia games – self-made and store-bought
- Playing cards

- Kindles, books
- *Travel Scrabble*

Packing for airport security

Our family has grown rather familiar with airport security over the years, and we now work the conveyer belt like a well-oiled machine. We each have a single soft neoprene zippered case in which to store our electronics - computer and charger, Kindle and mobile phone – which are held in the front compartments of our backpacks. These are easily pulled out and placed in the plastic bins to go through the x-ray machines.

To make things even easier, we wear pants that do not require belts. Slip-on shoes are preferred to laced boots and shoes because of the ease of taking them on and off.

Remember not to carry liquids more than 50ml per container, and never bring tweezers or Swiss Army Knives in your carry-on luggage. We have made these mistakes too many times!

PASSPORTS & VISAS

Here are some tips that might help you manage your passports and visas:

- If your passport will expire within six months, you may be denied entry into a country. Be sure there is plenty of time and space in each family members' passports.
- Check in advance which countries require visas pre-arranged, or if you can simply get one as you enter the country at an airport or border crossing. Occasionally, visas can be arranged over the internet – like for Australia - while other countries require travelers to go through the country's embassy or consulate.

Policies may differ according to which passport you hold. For example, rules do not apply equally to Canadians as they do to New Zealanders, as we found in Zimbabwe when I was required to pay considerably more for my visa than Sam was.

- If you are getting a visa at the border or airport you may be required to pay a fee. Bring enough cash to cover the cost in case credit cards are not accepted, or in case there are no bank machines around. If you don't have the local currency, most border crossings will accept US dollars.

- Some countries, like Indonesia, require visitors to pay a fee to exit the country, so make sure that you have cash on hand for that.

TELEPHONES

In today's world, travelers rely heavily on their smartphones to make travel arrangements, to keep in contact with family and friends, for emergency calls and to take photographs. Here are some tips that you might find helpful regarding bringing phones around the world:

- All four of us carried phones on our tour, primarily for taking photos, but also for texting and internet access. We were able to use our US-based mobile data service in virtually every country we visited, at no extra charge. Calls were charged at a per-minute rate, and the price varied according to the country we were calling from.

- As providers are always introducing new packages for international use, it would be worth your while to comparison shop.

- Call your provider's customer service department to get the details of their international package. Be ready with the list of countries you intend to visit, or simply might visit, so you can know in advance whether the plan will get you free coverage in those locations.

- One can usually purchase local SIM cards for phone calls but we generally find it easier to simply use Skype from our laptops, where WIFI is available. To call land-lines or mobile phones through Skype, upload money in advance either with your credit card or through PayPal.

Friends of ours prefer to communicate through apps like *Whatsap,* and *Viber* when they're abroad.

CREDIT & DEBIT CARDS

Credit cards are widely accepted in most countries today. We choose our cards based on the international transaction and translation charges. Given that banks are continuously changing their programs and policies with regards credit and debit card usage overseas, it is advisable that you shop for the best card to bring with you closer to your departure date. The following websites might help you comparison shop:

- Nerdwallet
- Creditcards.com
- The Simple Dollar
- Credit Karma
- The Points Guy
- WalletHub

Questions to consider when doing your credit and debit card research:

- *How much will I be charged for cash withdrawals overseas?*

- *What insurance benefits apply to purchases I make with the card? For instance, does using the card to rent a car entitle me to insurance coverage? Does it provide flight insurance?*
- *Are there points' benefits to using the card while travelling?*

One common travel problem that can be really frustrating is having your credit card blocked by your bank so you can't make transactions. This has happened to us a few too many times on previous trips, when our banks became suspicious about the variety of locations our transactions were being made from.

How can I prevent this from happening?

- Before the trip, let your credit card bank know where you will be and when. This usually requires a phone call to the customer service department. Have your itinerary on hand.
- Carry at least two, if not three, cards from different banks in case one of the cards has a hold put on it. We generally choose to separate the cards so if one wallet is stolen or lost we don't lose them all.
- Keep your credit card number and emergency telephone numbers on a thumb drive or in the Cloud, in case of emergency.

Reliable ATM machines can be found in most countries today, particularly in major cities and tourist areas. Whenever in doubt, make sure to get cash out at the airport upon arrival. Of course, always do your research in advance to know what the banking situation is in each location.

In some places in the developing world, low domination dollar bills can come in handy. We were advised to bring a stack of one dollar bills to Zimbabwe because they are valued more highly than the country's own unstable currency. But, certainly, not all developing countries share those concerns.

In most countries, restaurants and hotels tend to give a poorer exchange rate than what banks offer, so use the local currency as much as possible.

IMMUNIZATIONS

The following are just a few of the organizations found online that provide information about suggested vaccines for specific countries and regions. Ask your doctor where to get your immunizations, and be prepared for the cost. Insurance may or may not cover the expense, which can run high.

- Centers for Disease Control and Prevention – Traveler's Health
- The Travel Doctor
- Passport Health
- IAMAT – International Association of Medical Assistance for Travelers

Note that antimalarial pills are particularly expensive. The various options carry different side effects, so do your research before choosing which to go with.

MEDICAL INSURANCE

Be sure to choose medical insurance that covers all the activities you expect to participate in during your tour. Ours needed to cover risk-taking sports like kite boarding and whitewater rafting, as well as handling animals.

We actually did end up using the medical insurance. Declan got a stomach bug from working hands-on with the monkeys. The broad-spectrum antibiotic we brought with us did not help, so we went to a doctor in Hoedspruit, South Africa. The physician was excellent, he charged very little for his service and we did manage to get some of the payment reimbursed. We also took Declan to see a doctor in Bangkok for a mild fever, just to confirm it was not malaria. It wasn't. In both cases, we kept the receipts, dates and details about the treatment to forward to the insurance company upon our return.

Following those two successful clinic visits – one in Thailand and the other in small-town South Africa – Sam raised an interesting point. *There's something to be said for being in a country where doctors are familiar with the common ailments of the region. Had we been in Canada or the US, would the doctors have known how to diagnose malaria or a stomach bug caused by primates? Probably not.* Proper care can indeed be found in remote locations. Keep this in mind.

Getting reimbursed by insurance companies can be a slow, frustrating ordeal. I am not going to promote a specific travel insurance company here because my experiences with them have never been entirely satisfying. That said, travelling without insurance is never a wise choice.

5 TAKE-AWAYS

1. Pack light. Remember that you can always buy and replace items while you're traveling. Keep your important and valuable things in your carry-on bag, not in checked-in luggage. For extra items you won't need immediately, consider temporarily storing them to give you the freedom to live out of a compact-sized bag.

2. Make sure your passport is updated and has enough pages for stamps from all the countries you plan to visit. Research visa requirements and restrictions in advance, as policies differ from country to country.

3. Sign up for a mobile plan that will allow you to use your phone in every location you plan to visit.

4. Choose a credit card that is widely accepted and can earn you points while traveling. When you can't be sure that your cash card will be widely accepted in a place, take out a reasonable amount of cash from an airport ATM. Also, keep some local currency on hand for incidentals in places where credit and debit cards may not be widely used.

5. Research in advance of your trip which immunizations are recommended for every location you plan to visit. Note that these can be expensive, as can antimalarial pills.

Chapter 10
Managing The Home Front

Probably my least favorite part of this whole planning process was working out the mundane details of keeping our lives at home running in our absence. But to enjoy a worry-free vacation, it was crucial to get this right.

WHO IS GOING TO WATCH THE HOUSE AND PETS?

One of the first questions friends and family asked about our travel plans was *What are you going to do with your house?* It was a difficult question to answer as we owned rather than rented, so moving out and putting everything in storage was not a solution, although admittedly, we briefly considered it. To top it off, we had two much-loved cocker spaniels to be cared for. We were not willing to have them stay at a kennel, but it was not immediately obvious who might be able to watch them for several months.

It took time and a lot of effort to work out how we were going to deal with these obstacles, but in the end, as you will see, solutions were found and everything worked out well.

Professional Dog Sitters

We discovered *Rover.com* (formerly *DogVacay.com*) several years before, and continue to use the service whenever we leave town for short trips. The service represents thousands of dog sitters throughout North America who watch pets either in the pet owners' homes or their own. The sitters' locations, fees and backgrounds can be easily compared online, and reviews from past clients are provided. By paying the sitters' fees through the service, your pet is covered by insurance.

To date we have hired seven separate dog sitters in the Houston and Boston areas through the service and have been happy with every one of them. I would suggest doing your own online research to learn what similar pet sitting options are available in your area.

In the end, we chose not to go with this service for our gap year, however, because at $25-$40 a day per dog, we were looking at a minimum of $1500 a month for the two dogs. *Ouch!*

House & Pet Sitters

The ideal solution would have been to find someone willing to live in the house and watch the dogs. But who?

We usually go away for a few weeks every summer and have managed to find young, single people to watch the house and dogs. Other couples we know have invited their young colleagues to watch their homes. The chance to stay in an nice house in a different neighborhood can be a real treat for a young person still sleeping on a hard futon or an IKEA sofa-bed.

Of course, there is always a risk with inviting people to stay in your home, but over the years we have chosen this option on perhaps a dozen occasions and have not had a single bad experience. To limit our worries, we remove particularly precious items and hide them in the attic. Other options might include leaving the valuables at a trusted friend's home or in a commercial storage facility.

In the lead-up to our gap year, however, we couldn't find an appropriate tenant for that length of time. Our next option was a professional property management company.

Professional House Management

We narrowed our search down to a couple of local companies who were prepared to visit the house as often as we liked, at a cost of approximately $50 per visit. Their services included checking the house for intrusion, collecting mail, switching lights on and off so the place will look lived in, and bringing in contractors to deal with problems, such as plumbing, carpentry and pool care.

We came very close to choosing this option until we learnt something new.

Formal House Sitters

My cousin, Sandra, suggested that we invite her friend, Monica, to stay at the house and watch the dogs for us, as it was something she had been doing for couples all over the world since her retirement began. It turned out that she was able to come for most of the time we would be away. For the remaining two months, she suggested that we look at the Trusted House Sitters website – **trustedhousesitters.com.**

It turns out that thousands of people travel the world watching other people's houses and pets for free. The exchange helps travellers significantly reduce their accommodation costs while giving house and pet owners peace of mind.

I signed up for the service and within 24 hours had close to 30 responses from parties from all over the world willing to watch our house and dogs for us. Their responses came with bios and histories of past housesits they had done, including reviews from other home owners.

I narrowed the field down to five and began the interviewing process over Skype. Within 48 hours we found an ideal couple, Stephen and Claudia, who had recently retired from their responsible jobs in New Orleans. They were familiar with Houston and our neighborhood. Their son was living in Houston and they thought that a few months near their grandchildren would be great fun. They came with the added bonuses of owning a salt water pool like ours, so they knew how to manage it, and they had previously owned cocker spaniels themselves.

So, that's how we did it. The house and dogs were cared for by two sets of very responsible people. The dogs were well taken care of, the house was clean and in good order when we arrived back. Monica managed to deal with internet and air conditioning problems while we were away, and Stephen even planted a lovely herb garden for us. To this day, he and Claudia continue to house sit for us when we go out of town.

What's the moral of this story? Don't scratch any option off your list without giving it careful consideration. Also, keep your network open. You never know where great advice and support might come from.

INSTRUCTIONS FOR YOUR HOUSE SITTER

In preparation for our departure, I created an information pack to address most of the house sitters' questions and concerns. I began working on the list months in advance so it could be continuously added to as things came to mind. Here is a summary of what I included, which might help you begin your own list.

Essential information

- House contact details: House address, postal code, phone number
- Sam and my contact details: Phone number, email address, Facebook
- Emergency phone numbers of family and neighbors

- Emergency numbers - local police, hospitals, veterinarians and security service
- Important dates, approximating where we would be and when
- Contact information for trusted contractors (For any additional contactors, we gave the house sitters the authority to find their own through *Angie's List*.)

House

Specific instructions about the house:

- Garbage and recycling disposal – when, where and how
- Appliance instructions: Washer, dryer, dishwasher, vacuum, heater, air conditioner, security system, telephone, TV, electric gate/garage door, printer/scanner
- Services - gardener, grass cutter, pool service, pest control
- Mail – What to do with incoming mail.
- WIFI account and password
- Emergency house key
- Filters - where pre-purchased air filters were kept and when they needed to be changed

Neighborhood

I also drew up a list of local conveniences that might come in handy:

- Restaurants
- Supermarkets
- Gas stations
- Mechanics

- Emergency clinics
- Parks
- Dry cleaners
- Exercise venues
- Dog parks

HOUSE SITTER INFORMATION

While we travelled, we carried with us the following information about the house sitters:

- *Phone numbers*
- *Email addresses*
- *Home addresses*
- *License plate numbers (and photocopies of their driver's licenses)*
- *Social Security Numbers*
- *Emergency contact details – friends and family to call in case of emergency*

PET INSTRUCTIONS

- Veterinarian's contact details – phone, email, emergency phone number, address
- Feeding instructions
- Walking instructions – when and where
- Medication instructions, heartworm and flea prevention
- Sleeping arrangements
- Vaccination information - records provided (Pre-arranged annual vaccination appointments.)
- Dog grooming instructions and location

- Appointed person/s to watch pets in case sitter is not able to watch them for a certain length of time. (We nominated three people we had previously used through DogVacay.com)
- Other special instructions, for example, what to do on rainy days and in thunder storms.

Note that I purchased all dog food, medications (heartworm and flea prevention) and poop bags before departure.

HOUSESITTING CONTRACT

If you choose this type of housesitting arrangement, consider creating a contract that outlines the expectations of both parties.

We all signed a termination agreement, indicating what would happen if one party chose to end the arrangement early. It stated that 28 days notice would be required to vacate the premises, and then it would be turned over to either the homeowner or a nominated contact person.

Other key elements of such a contract might include how expenses incurred by the house sitter would be settled, as well as how damage caused by the house sitter would be covered.

You may choose to leave an envelope of money to cover incidentals and pre-arranged appointments, such as dog grooming and vaccinations. Our house sitters simply kept their receipts and we reimbursed them when we returned.

BILLS

Sam and I worked out which bills were likely to come through while we were away. In addition to standard monthly bills – like electricity, telephone and internet – we prepared for:

- Taxes – income, property
- Car registration
- Annual house security charges
- Life insurance
- Dog licenses
- School tuition for the following year

In most cases, we arranged automatic payment systems through our bank account. As for taxes, our accountant was given the authority to submit our tax returns. For the dogs' license renewal and security service renewal, both of which would be required half-way through our trip, I left checks in stamped and addressed envelopes for our house sitters to post at a specified time.

I suggest that where possible, cancel or freeze payments on services you won't be using while you're away, like gym memberships.

5 TAKE-AWAYS

1. If you need someone to watch your home during your gap year, begin by considering neighbors, friends and family who live in your area or who might be willing to temporarily move into our place. You might have luck asking a colleague who would appreciate living rent free for a while. Another alternative is hiring a professional house management company who can keep an eye on the place and manage any problems that arise.

2. If you simply need your pets watched in your absence, explore kennel options in your area or professional pet sitters advertised locally or through websites like *Rover.com*.

3. For families who need both their home and pets watched, and don't have acquaintances who can help, websites like *trustedhousesitters.com* provide an inexpensive solution.

4. Leave clear instructions about your home and pet to help your sitter manage any eventuality. Consider including a contract, signed by both parties, outlining expectations, roles and responsibilities.

5. Plan how you will have bills paid in your absence, including utilities, mortgage, annual taxes and so forth. Consider canceling or freezing payments on services you will not be using while you're away, like gym memberships and reserved parking fees.

Chapter 11
Keeping Your Memories Alive

Parents hope that their family gap years will lead to countless precious memories, but time does have the nasty habit of dimming the details and blurring the facts in our minds. We may recall pleasant feelings that a place brought us, and brief flashes of standout experiences, but gradually we will lose more than we remember.

What can you do about that? How can you keep the memories alive for years and years to come? Here are some ideas.

WRITING

Each of our family members kept a journal. Evenings in our New Zealand camper van, lazing in hammocks under banana trees in Vietnam, and tucked into our sleeping bags on top of our truck in Namibia were all perfect times to write.

For Sam and me, it came easily. Rarely in our adult lives had we so much time to indulge our creativity and self-expression, and we did so through journaling and creative writing.

For the kids, keeping a journal was one of the key elements of their on-the-road schooling, but the activity gradually became something they did for enjoyment.

Many of the short stories we wrote came directly from the experiences we were having, with a touch of creative license thrown in. Some of the kids' creative works were on completely unrelated topics, but echoed their sense of freedom to just write. One can almost feel the warm tropical sunshine coming through in their words.

Important Note - *Free from distractions*

During those months on the road, we did not have TV or computer games that would have been the kids' obvious go-to activities back home. Our evenings were spent reading and talking, and the kids spent a lot of time entertaining themselves through their own creative outlets. Some of what they produced became the archives of our family gap year.

SCHOOLING ASSIGNMENTS

As part of their schooling, the kids developed a portfolio of research essays, brochures, newsletters, PowerPoint presentations and video documentaries about our travels that we will keep forever.

DECLAN INDULGING IN SOME CREATIVE INSPIRATION. NAMIB DESERT, NAMIBIA

ART

Ever since Declan was small, he would carry a pad of paper, a selection of mechanical pencils and an eraser wherever he went, just in case he had a flash of inspiration to be captured. The pages were filled with cartoons, inventions or systems designs, and short story ideas. This tradition continued throughout our family gap year.

Scout and I also enjoy drawing while we're traveling, and our summers in France always include painting water colors of ancient buildings and local flowers. These pictures represent summer to us, slowness and all that's deliciously French.

PHOTOS & ALBUMS

To say we took a lot of photos on the trip is a bit of an understatement. At last count, we had over 4000 to sort through when we got home. And I'm so glad we did! They captured the beauty of the places, the things we did and our feelings at each moment. I still can't get enough of browsing through them even now. We all have the photos on our phones, and they come up on our laptop screen savers and desktops, but where we most enjoy looking at them is in the albums I created when we got home.

For the past 10 years, I have presented the family with an annual album, including photos, the kids' artwork, some funny quotes and awards, all created through the online **Blurb.com** website. I used the same site for our trip albums, including photos, journal entries, creative stories, a selection of the kids' learning assignments, drawings and a long list of inside jokes that keep us laughing.

One of the gap year albums focuses on South-East Asia, the second on New Zealand and Europe, and the third on Africa. I had three copies of each printed – one sits on our coffee table today, and the other two have been stored away for the kids to have when they grow up.

We flick through these whenever we feel nostalgic. . . which is often.

Our three precious gap year albums.

Chapter 12
Final Thoughts

Greeted at the door by two desperately excited cocker spaniels, we collapsed onto the sofa with our bags left in a pile by the door. The kids immediately began to list American foods they wanted to stock the fridge with. Declan turned on his favorite *Seinfeld* episode. Scout began texting her friends madly, announcing her return. We were home. But we were different, and I dare say, improved - each of us in different ways.

Life changes

I struggled to write this chapter. My reflections were so deep and personal that it didn't seem appropriate to make them public. Instead, I spent long hours working through my thoughts about what we had done, how we felt about each part of the tour and how we had grown closer. It was important to do and to share with each other. These private musings are now secure in our family albums.

Still, it wouldn't be right to not include a brief glimpse into the changes we noticed. We've gone this far together.

In no time flat, Declan was back into the groove with his community of like-minded science enthusiasts. Their computer games had changed, but their keenness had not waned. What had clearly changed, however, was his self-confidence. Our son, who had always preferred his own company to anyone else's, immediately began expanding his social base to include a far wider range of kids.

He stood taller, felt stronger – physically and metaphorically – and he was noticeably more inclined to put himself out there.

Can I attribute all of that to the tour? I don't know. Perhaps that's a natural stage in the life of a 14-year old. But the change was so dramatic, such a stark contrast from the boy who got on that plane to Moscow months earlier, that it's hard not to imagine that the tour didn't give it a firm nudge down that path.

Scout changed in terms of her interests. The tour allowed her to embrace her innate fearlessness. She had done so many things that most 12-year olds could only dream of, or couldn't even imagine, and with this change came a natural shift in her social circle towards kids with similar values and senses of adventure. It was not an easy re-entry for our girl. Continuous change and stimulation that comes with an around-the-world tour can be addictive, and traditional schooling can be monotonous. Her solace came from knowing that this was not the last time she would travel the world. Not at all.

Sam came back to a new and improved job. He approached his work-life with a far more relaxed attitude, taking the pressures and deadlines in his stride. It's as though experiencing so much of the world reminded him that day-to-day trivia shouldn't be allowed to obfuscate what really matters. He is now allowing himself more time to relax, to read and play guitar. And he's sure to remind me regularly of our long-term plans of returning to Africa where he'll get involved in water supply efforts in Namibia and I'll work to help women and children in need. It's his new dream – our dream.

A lot of my time since our return has been focused on compiling this book series, and developing online courses for likeminded parents. There's something so nice about sharing the knowledge I've accumulated over the years. In a small way, these avenues allow me to relive our adventures again and again.

My lifelong dream to take an extended tour around the world with my family has been fulfilled, but not extinguished. I still can't quite convince myself that this is the last time we're going to do this. Now that we know how doable, and wonderful, it can be, there's little to justify not heading off at least one more time, while the kids are still keen to travel with *ol' Mom and Dad.*

My mind drifts to our next itinerary – to Myanmar, Nepal, Rwanda, Israel, Mongolia and back to southern Africa. A convoluted list, perhaps, but now I know we can make it happen. Maybe I'll see you there!

POST-READING QUESTIONAIRE:

What's your current thinking about your family gap year adventure?

1. *What ideas do you now have for your family gap year? Do any locations or activities stand out in your mind?*

2. *What would be the ideal length of time for your family gap year tour? Why?*

3. *What do you imagine you and your family would get out of a gap year experience? What could it do for you? How might it change each of you?*

4. *Which words describe your current feelings about planning a family gap year experience?*

   Excited   *Doubtful*

   Overwhelmed   *Expectant*

   Nervous   *Ready*

   Hopeful   *Anything else?*

5. *What do you feel are the greatest obstacles to your family gap year adventure? How will you overcome them?*

6. *On a scale of one to ten, how ready are you to grab the kids and go? Not ready! 1 2 3 4 5 6 7 8 9 10 Let's go!*

Have your feelings about your family gap year changed as a result of reading this book?

What information did you find helpful? Do you have any additional questions that you would like help answering? By logging onto my website familygapyears.com (Note there is an "s" on years because once you've done it, you'll want to do it again!), you can pose your question to me, or share your ideas with other adventurous parents. Or you could leave your review on Amazon.

If the desire to move ahead with your travel plans is still there, but you would appreciate the chance to bounce ideas around with like-minded parents, consider joining one of our facilitated **Family Travel Coaching Groups**, found on the same website or email me at familygapyears@gmail.com.

Happy travels!

Taryn

ABOUT THE AUTHOR

Taryn Ash was raised by Canadian parents who taught her from a young age that travel was the reason why people earned money. Europe was her family's destination of choice when she was a child, but by her early 20's, when she and her friend strapped on their packs and headed for Tokyo to work, she was hooked on Asia. Together they spent several glorious months exploring the continent, unaware that Taryn would end up spending most of her adult life in the Far East.

She returned to Japan two more times, first to study Asian politics and business at Kansai Gaidai University, and then to teach English and international studies at a rural high school. She went on to study demography at Jilin University, China, before becoming a college lecturer in Singapore. One month in, she met her Kiwi soul mate and future travel partner, Sam, who was backpacking his way around the world at the time.

They dropped their bags, got married and spent the next 13 years growing their family together in Singapore, and traveling the world during their spare time. *(Close to 50 countries, at last count!)* Then it was off to Beijing, where she, Sam and their two kids, Declan and Scout, spent five fascinating years.

Taryn built her business in organizational behaviour and workplace curriculum design. Recently, more of her time is directed toward executive coaching, with a side focus on transition coaching for expats.

Taryn, Sam and the kids currently reside in Boston, and spend their summers (and most spare cash) on restoring their ancient house in their French village, Roquecor.

CONTRIBUTORS

One of the nicest parts about writing this book was gathering ideas from my community of well-traveled family and friends. I would like to thank them here and let you, the reader, know a bit about the experts who shared their wisdom in these pages.

Daniela Draugelis is a global nomad, daughter of Lithuanian immigrants, raised in Argentina, and has lived in Germany, the US, China and Indonesia. She, her husband, Gailius, and two sons have travelled extensively through Asia, Europe and North America. Daniela loves to learn about new cultures through travel, explore the great outdoors, enjoy good food, smiling faces and blue skies. Daniela recently relocated from Jakarta, Indonesia to Washington, DC.

Seth Raman & Alison Fox were raised in traveling families, and between them have toured numerous countries throughout Asia, Europe, Central and South America, as well as across the United States. Both teachers, they hope to instill that love of exploring different cultures in their children, and love seeing their daughters expand their understanding of the world while recognizing the similarities to be found among all people, regardless of geography. They currently live in Chicago.

Jennifer Sachs was raised in Baltimore and arrived in Beijing over 25 years ago where she set up home with her beloved Beijing husband, Li Wei. She owns a successful school and tutoring center in the Chinese capital. She was raised by two world travelers who hooked her on cruising at the tender age of 8, and with her three boys in tow, she has cruised the waters around Russia, Japan, Cambodia, Vietnam, Thailand, Mexico, Canada, and the U.S. and looks forward to many more miles at sea. Jennifer continues to make China her home.

Debbie Vopni is a Canadian who headed off to experience the world in her 20's with all her possessions crammed into two hockey bags *(Truly Canadian!)*. For the next twenty years, she lived in HK, Thailand, London, Singapore and Dubai, and then returned to Canada with a husband, three kids, two containers and her heart full of beautiful memories and adventures in Asia, Europe and the Middle East. She's looking forward to continuing her journey wherever her shoes and the wind take her. Debbie currently lives in Edmonton, Canada.

Tina Ryan is an Australian dentist who lives in Singapore with her Filipino husband, Napoleon, and their three children. As a family, they have travelled extensively around Asia, Europe, Australia and the US. Tina believes that traveling with kids is one of the best ways to expand their minds. In additional to all the amazing educational benefits, she loves how travel allows the family to spend quality time together while creating priceless memories.

Vivian Nazari is a dentist, born in Canada and grew up in Iran, attending an IB school founded by Americans, until she moved to England after the Iranian revolution. She has also lived in France, China and the US. She and her American husband lived and worked in England and China for several years and have travelled extensively throughout Southeast Asia, Africa, Europe, the Middle East and the US with their three children, starting from when they were as young as three months old. She is proud to have instilled in them the belief that they are global citizens. She loves to see new places, but Mongolia, Kenya and Rajasthan have special places in her heart. Vivian currently lives in Washington, DC.

Katrina Brandon is a widely-published expert on the human dimensions of biodiversity conservation. Spending her childhood in Costa Rica and South Florida led to her interest in conservation, especially for reefs and rainforests, and for indigenous and rural people. A mom of three grown kids, all (with her husband who is an environmental economist) lived in Argentina, travelling widely around the Americas, and then in China, exploring SE Asia. She is thrilled that as adults, all three speak Spanish fluently, have strong international interests, love travel, hiking, and exploring new cultures and countries, and feel their well-stamped passport is their most valuable possession. Katrina currently lives in Washington, DC

Erica Hodge Walpole is originally from New Jersey, but as a young adult headed first for the Caribbean and then to Asia where she met her Australian husband and gave birth to their two sons. Erica has travelled extensively in the United States, the Caribbean, Europe, Asia and Australia both independently and with her family. She loves seeing new places through the eyes of her children and seeing what stands out to them during their travels. She believes the experiences have made them deeper thinkers and are more open-minded. Erica treasures the time spent researching, planning and getting excited for family trips together. She and her family currently reside in Atlanta, Georgia.

Claire Cuccio was interested in transnational culture and the Other from her earliest years. Her first extended encounter began in Japan where her passion for the written language and its range of expressive forms culminated in a doctorate in Japanese literature. She also encountered a partner there who shared an enduring interest in East Asia. Together they passed on Asian languages and a cross-cultural lifestyle to their two children from Taiwan to Mainland China, Japan and back to China. Currently based in Washington, DC, Claire works as an independent writer and researcher on East Asian print and papermaking, traditional artisans and hand craft, and contemporary print and paper artists, all informed by her experiences of collaborating with individuals on the ground in Asia. She is looking forward to their next family move to Nepal where she will resume this person-to-person contact with makers of the Asian world.

Sarah Mavrinac is an American academic and award-winning social entrepreneur. Her focus has long been on women's economic empowerment in the developing world. More recently, she dedicates her time to issues related to raising special needs kids. She and her Canadian husband raised their two kids in France, Singapore and Abu Dhabi. They have enjoyed traveling in Asia, the Middle East, North America and Africa, and currently live between the UAE and Portugal.

Scout Ash-Dale is a Canadian-New Zealander, whose feels at home in Singapore, Beijing, Canada, New Zealand and France, which she explains in her TedX Talk *Third Culture Kid* https://www.youtube.com/watch?v=S6OwjUA5NTY. She dreams of one day living in Africa and working with children and wildlife.

Declan Ash-Dale is a Canadian-New Zealander, born and raised in Singapore until entering elementary school in China. His middle and high school years are being spent in Houston and Boston. He travelled to 24 countries by the age of 15, but his heart belongs to Bali, Singapore and Whistler, Canada.

 **Sam Dale** was born and raised in New Zealand. Following graduate school, he set off to travel the world, which landed him in Singapore, where he met his future travel partner and wife, Taryn. He sold his airline ticket, got a job and spent the next 20 years living in Singapore, China and the US. Originally a journalist, Sam now works in the energy industry. He and his family have travelled extensively through Asia, Europe, North American, New Zealand, Australia and Africa. Although he currently lives between the US and France, his home is wherever his family find themselves on any given day.

ACKNOWLEDGEMENTS

There are many other people that I would like to recognize for influencing this book and allowing me to mention them in these pages: Fay and Wayne Ash, Michael Ash, Ady and Peter Dale, Shannon Webster, Michael Job, Emma Jenkins, Billy Buchsbaum, Sandy Baker, Silke von Eynern, Georgio Schwaiger, Ms. Grace, Ms. Nyathi, Mabel Gajisan, Angel Gajisan, Romer Gajisan, Steve and Claudia Braud, Cheryl-Ann Gajisan, Kimberly Cooper, Kristie Zamora Becker, Ethan Brown, Isabelle Perez-Gore and Tim Gore, Sandy Baker, Dan Murray, Monica Schimanke and Uatiza (Michael)Hepute.

For more information about Taryn's travel-related books, online training and coaching resources, go to familygapyears.com.

OTHER TITLES BY TARYN ASH

SCHOOLING-THROUGH-TRAVEL:
How the World Became our Kids' Classroom

In writing this book, Taryn drew from her 25-years experience as an award winning curriculum designer, college lecturer, high school teacher and stakeholder in a tutoring center in China.

Printed in Great Britain
by Amazon